THE WEST COAST TRAIL

AND OTHER GREAT HIKES

8th Revised and Expanded Edition

THE WEST COAST TRAIL

AND OTHER GREAT HIKES

THE JUAN DE FUCA TRAIL

THE CARMANAH–WALBRAN TRAILS

NITINAT LAKES

TIM LEADEM
for the Sierra Club of British Columbia

THE
MOUNTAINEERS

GREYSTONE BOOKS
Douglas & McIntyre
Vancouver/Toronto

Published in Canada by
Greystone Books
A division of Douglas & McIntyre
1615 Venables Street
Vancouver, British Columbia
V5L 2H1

CANADIAN CATALOGUING IN PUBLICATION DATA

Leadem, Tim
    The West Coast Trail and other great hikes

    Previous eds. by the Sierra Club of Western Canada
    ISBN 1-55054-614-7

    1. Hiking—British Columbia—West Coast Trail—Guidebooks.
    2. Hiking—British Columbia—Nitinat Lake Region—
    Guidebooks. 3. Trails—British Columbia—Nitinat Lake
    Region—Guidebooks. 4. West Coast Trail (B.C.)—Guidebooks.
    5. Nitinat Lake Region (B.C.)—Guidebooks. I. Sierra Club of
    Western Canada. II. Title.
    GV199.44.C22B749 1998   917.11'2   C97-911097-1

Originated by Greystone Books and published simultaneously in the United States of America by The Mountaineers.

  Published in the United States by
The Mountaineers
1001 SW Klickitat Way, #201
Seattle, WA 98134

LIBRARY OF CONGRESS CATALOGUING IN PUBLICATION DATA

A catalog record for this book is available at the Library of Congress.
ISBN 0-89886-536-0 (United States)
US seventh edition ISBN: 0-89886-399-6

Cover photography by David Nunuk/First Light
Text design and composition by Val Speidel
Cover design by Isabelle Swiderski
Printed and bound in Canada by Best Book Manufacturers
Printed on acid-free paper ∞

Contents

Preface to the 8th Edition

I T HAS BEEN TWENTY-FIVE YEARS since this guide was first published. That's a fairly long stretch for us humans but a minuscule passage of time for the ancient trees of the rain forest. When I first hiked the trail in 1974 in the company of my brother, I was in awe of the sheer beauty of this spot where crashing surf met rocky shore and where coastal fog hugged the mystical apparitions of Sitka spruce. Time has not diminished that sense of the wild, but the solitude of the trail is becoming more difficult to experience. Others, more eloquently than I could ever hope to, have waxed lyrical on the meaning of wilderness to our ever more technocratical society. When I stand in a grove of cedars and experience the calm of just being there, I know that it is essential to preserve such spots for those who will walk in their shade and breathe the aromatic essence of them years from now.

The lessons that conservationists have learned over the last two and a half decades can be distilled into this message: to preserve a place, one must first discover it and then promote it. For it is only through public awareness that one can hope to turn the tide of development and clear-cutting. But therein lies the paradox—to preserve a wild spot, it

< Sombrio Beach. ADRIAN DORST

must often be opened to human scrutiny in order to obtain the will to preserve it. And often some of the wild is rubbed away in the process.

We need the wild places for our souls—the churning, swirling sea as it shoots and swells up surge channels, the liquid emerald of a stream running through a rocky gorge, the glint of the sun off a tiny fern in the dank humus of the forest floor. And perhaps we need them just to be and not necessarily to be there for us. The myriad species that make up the forest ecosystem can survive without us quite nicely. And there should be such places on this globe where humans don't dare to tread.

So by all means enjoy these hikes. Take in their incredible beauty and inexhaustible wonder. But leave these sacred places as you found them. Or better still, do your part to ensure that there are other wild places that we may know in our hearts if not with our eyes.

Acknowledgements

THE FIRST EDITION OF THIS BOOK was a cooperative effort of members of the Sierra Club of British Columbia who loved the trail and fought hard to save it. Humphrey Davy, Jim Hamilton, Hugh Murray, Karen McNaught, Ric Careless, John Willow and Gordy Price all pioneered the West Coast Trail and Nitinat Lake area in order to promote the area and conserve it.

The Juan de Fuca Trail received similar efforts from Sierra Club members Bruce Hardy, Chris Nation, John Newcombe and Greg Darms. The preservation of the Carmanah Valley owes much to the hard work of the Western Canada Wilderness Committee. A large chunk of the Walbran Valley has been saved through the combined efforts of several environmental groups, including the Carmanah Forestry Society.

This edition replaces the text of the previous editions, which was prepared by Tim Leadem, Bruce Hardy, John Twigg and Ken Farquharson. Photographs were taken by Bo Martin, Adrian Dorst and Tim Leadem. Maps were prepared by Cathy Riley and Tim Leadem.

The author thanks the employees and staff of Pacific Rim National Park and B.C. Parks for their many helpful comments and suggestions. Similar gratitude is due to all of the many hikers along the way who offered commentary. To hiking companions past and present who shared the scenery and sometimes the travails of the trail, may the path rise up to greet you and may the wind be ever at your back.

Since conditions along these trails are constantly changing, neither the author nor the publisher guarantees the accuracy of the information in this book. You must allow for the unexpected.

CHAPTER ONE

Introduction

F OR OVER ONE HUNDRED YEARS there has been at least some semblance of a trail along the west coast of Vancouver Island between Pachena and Port Renfrew. The trail was first hacked out of the wilderness in 1889 for a telegraph line connecting Victoria with Bamfield, the western terminus of the first transpacific telegraph cable, which was meant to connect the British Empire. The old cable station in Bamfield is now the Marine Biological Station in Bamfield, which is the centre for study into marine biology and ocean science for five western Canadian universities.

In 1906 the wreck of the SS *Valencia*, just north of the mouth of the Klanawa River, took the lives of 126 people. After this wreck, the federal government made improvements to the rough path put up by the stringers of the telegraph line so that it could serve as a lifesaving trail for survivors of shipwrecks. It then became known as the Life Saving Trail, or the Shipwrecked Mariners Trail. Over the last century, a number of ships have foundered along this stretch of the coast, giving it the name the Graveyard of the Pacific. In 1911 the trail was designated a public highway, and the federal government took on the responsibility of maintaining it. Cabins were also built at various strategic locations, and lineworkers were stationed in them to patrol the trail and the telegraph line to insure that it was kept in operation. Remains of one of these cabins may be seen today along the trail at the Klanawa River.

As long ago as 1926, when the land in British Columbia seemed infinite, the recreation potential of the Nitinat Lake and the coast was recognized, and a park reserve was established. This reserve was lifted in 1947 because the federal government considered the region too remote for recreation. A struggle broke out within the forest industry for control of the land base. First the area was set up as the Clayoquot Cutting Circle, where small, independent operators could work. But the major logging companies had their own plans for the area. After World War II, trail conditions had deteriorated and the federal government temporarily abandoned the trail in 1954. Interest in the trail was rekindled in the 1960s, when members of the Sierra Club began to hike and upgrade the trail. The Sierra Club also began intensive lobbying to have the trail set aside as a national park. In response, the federal government began to upgrade portions of the trail. Improvements to the trail continued in the 1970s—mostly to the northern section of the trail. The upgrade of the trail was completed by 1983. The trail was formally established as the West Coast Trail Unit of Pacific Rim National Park in 1993.

Since this book was first written, in 1972, the West Coast Trail and environs have changed in several ways. At that time the area had not yet been conserved as parkland and was still remote, attracting primarily rugged backpackers who wanted to enjoy a wilderness experience. Rugged backpackers still hike the trail, but they are joined by families and by retirees who now have the leisure to enjoy outdoor activities.

Responding to the increased use of the trail and to the shift in the type of people hiking the trail, the Canadian Parks Service carried out a program of repairs to the West Coast Trail in the 1980s to eliminate many of the obvious dangers and inconveniences. In the 1990s the provincial government added large tracts of land in the Carmanah-Walbran watersheds as well as a southern extension to the West Coast Trail—the Juan de Fuca Marine Trail. The result has been a vast increase in the number of hikers and back country users of the area.

The West Coast Trail is relatively easy to hike from Pachena Bay to Walbran Creek. From Walbran Creek to Port Renfrew the hike is relatively safe but not necessarily easy; there are still dangers for the unwary hiker. Whereas the trail is still a challenge to the average hiker, it is no longer the true wilderness it once was. For many, this change is distress-

The Graveyard of the Pacific, West Coast Trail. ADRIAN DORST

ing because it removes a challenge that cannot easily be replaced; for others, however, it means the opportunity to experience an area they may have been reluctant to enter a few years ago. One negative aspect of change, though, is the increased spoiling of the land caused by the carelessness or ignorance of hikers uneducated in trail courtesy and camping etiquette. This problem will only get worse unless every hiker develops a personal sense of stewardship for the land.

This new edition has been written with two main purposes: (1) to help hikers of all ages and all levels of experience and ability enjoy the coastal trails of Vancouver Island, and (2) to convey the urgent need to protect the quality of experience that these trails offer. Since the number of hikers allowed on the West Coast Trail each summer is now restricted, many who wish to experience the beauty of coastal old-growth forest where it meets crashing surf or a clear stream may be precluded from trekking the trail. Thus, this edition has been expanded to include other areas adjacent to the West Coast Trail and Pacific Rim National Park. There are two new chapters, one on hiking the Juan de Fuca Marine Trail, now a provincial park, and the other on hiking in the new provincial park of the Carmanah–Walbran.

PERSONAL CAUTIONS

Before hiking any of the trails described in this book, you should be aware of some of the potential problems you may encounter.

1. Respect the sea. It is unbelievably powerful and can catch you unawares. The worst danger is from an occasional freak Pacific swell— or rogue waves, as they are sometimes called—tumbling up a surge channel or rising dramatically over rocks or the sandstone shelf. People have been plucked off rocks and carried out to sea by these sudden swells. A particularly dangerous spot is Nitinat Narrows, where you may be temporarily marooned if there is no one available to ferry you across. Very fast currents mixed with ocean breakers have caused many deaths there. In fact, all of Nitinat Lake is noted for dangerously high winds and waves. Finally, be aware and wary of tides. More than one camper has set up a tent well away from the sea at low tide, only to find tent and gear awash and afloat in the middle of the night. Another serious situation is hiking the shore at low tide and finding your progress barred by a cliff or surge channel and your return barred by an incoming tide. See Chapter 8 for a discussion of tide tables.

2. Respect rocks, cliffs, slippery rocks and logs and the sandstone shelf. There are hazards on all parts of these trails. Slips on logs or rocks may result in serious injuries that require evacuation. On some parts of the coastal trails, you are one step away from a long drop. If your hiking boots lack good traction, the dangers are multiplied. A heavy pack can also increase the danger of a fall.

When Parks Canada conducted extensive trail renovations in the 1980s, many of the rotten boardwalks on the West Coast Trail were replaced with new ones. These boardwalks are now showing the inevitable signs of wear, however. At the time of publication, Parks Canada had just tendered a contract for maintenance work. This work is long overdue. Many boardwalks and ladders are broken, with missing boards or rungs. To cross rotting boadwalks, step on two planks at the same time or walk along the log supports. If the walk is tilted, you should either walk off the boards if there is space or walk along the lower edge of the walkway, nearer to the ground. If the boards are slippery, it is safest to walk off the boards altogether. Maintaining a medium speed allows you to keep going forward instead of down should a board break.

3. Be prepared for rain. Even during the summer months, you may encounter bad weather on the west coast of Vancouver Island. Within hours a front may move in, bringing cold air, strong winds and torrential rains. Rain gear is one of your most important pieces of equipment and should be adequate to keep you and your sleeping bag dry. A tent with waterproof fly is a necessity. You should know the meaning of and the symptoms of hypothermia, a condition that can sneak up on you and is the leading cause of death among amateur hikers. Hypothermia is discussed in Chapter 8.

4. Be properly equipped. Once on these trails, you may be some distance from the end and any guaranteed source of supplies. You should be self-sufficient, with enough food to last the duration of your planned trip. Suggested equipment is listed in Chapter 7.

5. Comfortable, sturdy hiking boots are essential. Next to rain gear and a waterproof tent, they are the most critical items for safe hiking.

6. Carry a water container. There are parts of the trail where, in a dry summer, you might hike for several hours without finding potable water.

7. Carry a stove for cooking, since heavy rainfalls may make it difficult to start a fire. Fires along coastal trails are restricted to the beach area. A stove is also required for all camping in the Carmanah–Walbran Provincial Park, since campfires are not allowed in wilderness campsites.

8. Carry a first-aid kit.

9. The Canadian Parks Service at Pacific Rim National Park (PRNP) strongly recommends against hiking the West Coast Trail from October 1 through April 15. There is no scheduled ferry service across Nitinat Narrows. Conditions along the trail are likely to be severe, and the PRNP does not provide rescue services on the trail during the off-season. Those who do decide to hike in the off-season and require search-and-rescue services must be prepared to wait for help and to pay for any rescue operation, including the cost of helicopter evacuation. The same warning applies to hiking any of the other coastal trails during the winter or off-season.

10. The PRNP now requires a West Coast Trail use permit for all

overnight use on the West Coast Trail. Without such a permit, you will not be able to hike the West Coast Trail. The acquisition and reservation system for permits is discussed in Chapter 6.

11. These trails should not be your first hiking experience. You will encounter most or all of the following: mud, slippery logs, slippery rocks, washouts, high streams, high tides, sudden ocean surges, dropoffs, steep banks, windfalls, overgrown sections, darkness, high winds and torrential rains. If you are not comfortable with encountering any of these elements, you should probably not attempt these hikes. If, however, you are willing to rough it and adapt to what the weather may throw your way, by all means prepare well and go ahead.

Reading this guide is not a substitute for experience. Remember the trail conditions change every year. Winter storms topple trees across the trails or wash out portions of the trails. Many of the trails in the Carmanah–Walbran are only for experienced hikers who are used to rough trail conditions and bushwhacking through dense forest.

ENVIRONMENTAL CAUTIONS

If nine thousand people pass through an area in a season and each person does a little damage to the environment, the result is a lot of damage. If each hiker does no damage, however, the result will be no damage. It is easy to visit an area, use it and enjoy being there but leave behind no sign of your visit.

1. Pack out all of your garbage. The rule for all wilderness hiking is: "If you can pack it in, you can carry it out." This rule applies to all tin cans, food packages, bottles, clothing, plastic bags and polyethylene sheets. Burying your garbage is not a solution, given the number of people who use the trail and the non-biodegradable nature of most garbage. Burnable garbage should be thoroughly burned, both for aesthetic reasons and to avoid attracting animals to campsites. Human solid wastes should be buried or deposited in the intertidal flush zone. Use the outhouses provided by parks staff, but do not put garbage in them.

2. When setting up your campsite, use an area that obviously has already been used. Do not hack a new site out of the bush. If you are beach camping, camp below the winter high-tide line and, of course, well above the summer high-tide line.

3. Confine bathing and using soap for washing dishes to areas downstream of camping and intake of water supply. Use biodegrad-

able soap or, better yet, no soap at all. Instead use sand and small rocks to scour pots and pans.

4. Respect all private lands. The main private lands in the national park belong to First Nations and are clearly marked as Indian reserve lands. Native guardians patrol all reserve lands. No camping or trespassing is allowed on these lands—you must remain on the trail. Over the years lands and buildings belonging to Native people have been vandalized and damaged. All reserve lands are clearly marked on the maps in this book.

5. Remember that large groups have a greater environmental impact on the trail than small groups and a greater social impact on other campers. Parks staff restricts group size to ten. Many of the more popular camping spots along the coastal trails, such as Tsusiat, become quite crowded. In these areas it is important to recognize that some hikers may have a different schedule for hiking than you. Some may rise early to catch the low tide; others may want to sleep in to recover from the inevitable aches and pains of backpacking. Keep others in mind and keep the noise level down when you are in camping areas.

6. Refrain from taking any sea life, such as mussels or clams, for personal consumption. In addition to the problem with red tide (discussed in Chapter 9), sea life is not easily replenished when so many hikers are travelling along the coast.

CHAPTER TWO

Hiking the
West Coast Trail

THE TRAIL MAY BE HIKED IN either direction or even from the middle at Nitinat Narrows to either of the two trailheads. Traditionally, the hike has been described from the south or the Port Renfrew trailhead to the northern terminus at Bamfield. Many people prefer to hike the trail in this direction to get the southern, more difficult part over with when they are still fresh. There are others, however, who prefer to hike the easier northern section while their packs are heavy and full of food and to break into the trail gradually. The decision is yours. For the sake of tradition, this book describes the trail as one proceeds from southeast to northwest. Where hikers proceeding in the opposite direction need to be aware of a particular problem, I have included this fact in the notes and trail description that follow.

Further information on access to the trailheads at Bamfield, Port Renfrew and Nitinat is given in Chapter 6. Before beginning the trail, you must report to one of the trailhead information centres to pick up your trail use permit and to complete a mandatory orientation session given by a PRNP staff member. Up-to-date information on trail conditions, on any known problem areas and on the tidal conditions you can

< Sandstone shelf, West Coast Trail. ADRIAN DORST

expect for the duration of your trip is dispensed by knowledgeable staff at the centres. You will also be shown a fifteen-minute video presentation that describes what you may expect along the way. If you wish to get an early start in the morning, you should pick up your permit and complete your orientation the day before you begin your hike.

To enter the trail at the southern end, you will need a boat; the Gordon River is too deep and wide to wade. On the eastern side of the river, the land belongs to the Pacheenaht Indian Band. The present operator of the ferry service across the Gordon River is Butch Jack, a member of the Pacheenaht Band. He will ferry you across the river from the reserve and, if you wish, pick you up from the government dock located seaward of the Port Renfrew Hotel in the townsite. For specific information on ferry routes and options, see Chapter 6. The PRNP advises that beginning in 1998, the ferry service will not drop off or pick up at Thrasher Cove and thus all hikers will start and finish at the Gordon River.

From the Gordon River to Thrasher Cove, the trail stays in the forest, well away and up from the coastline. The coastal route is impassable because of the presence of cliffs. Any difficulties you encounter on the southern part of the trail will mainly depend on the weather. If it has been rainy, you should expect mud of varying depths, and all log crossings and boardwalks will be slippery. The hiking is mostly on flat ground or gentle up-and-down terrain. When you pass the old donkey engine, a relic of earlier logging, you will be about halfway to Thrasher Cove. Note that the forest around the southern portion of the trail is second growth and contains dense underbrush that is not found on other parts of the trail. From the halfway point to Thrasher Cove the climbs become steeper. At several points there are openings in the forest that may yield excellent views of Port San Juan and the distant Olympic Mountains in Washington.

A good campsite is found about 5 metres (16 feet) off the main trail at its highest point; follow a huge log and an old logging cable. There is room for at least four tents. This campsite has a fine view of the ocean and the Olympic Mountains. The nearest water is about 150 metres (500 feet) away, however, at a stream that may run dry in summer and that lies at the bottom of a steep path. So if you plan to camp at this site, fill your water bottles (and treat or filter that water) at one of the streams after passing the donkey engine.

< Olympic Mountains viewed from
Juan de Fuca Trail. TIM LEADEM

After the high point, the trail
drops steeply to a small creek called
Log Jam Creek, with a bridge across
it. After the creek you reach an
intersection. Thrasher Cove is to
the left down a steep trail with a
series of ladders. Face inward
when using the ladders and make
sure of your footing on the sometimes muddy or slippery rungs. Excellent camping awaits at Thrasher Cove, which has a good water supply
from Hobbs Creek.

The trail from Thrasher Cove to 150 Yard Creek can be slow going.
At low tide you can hike along the shore to the west of Thrasher Cove.
At first it is slow and tedious travel among slippery, algae-covered boulders, but after you reach the sandstone shelf you can pick up speed.
Just before you encounter the sandstone shelf you will have to scramble through a landslide consisting of large boulders. There are some
beautiful sea caves to the east of Owen Point, which are well worth
exploring if you have the time to do so before high tide. Keep in mind
that you must reach the first beach access trail near 150 Yard Creek
before the sandstone shelf floods at high tide.

The campsite at 150 Yard Creek is small and extremely wet, but it is
a useful place to camp if you don't have time to make it to Camper Bay.

A side trail a few minutes out of 150 Yard campsite leads to a rocky
shelf at the shoreline. At low tide it is possible to walk along the shelf,
but be sure the tide will stay out long enough to allow you to reach the
next access point leading to the main trail. One difficulty with hiking
along the sandstone shelf is that in several areas sea chasms or surge
channels break the shelf. It is usually possible to outflank these by
using rough bypass trails. It is impossible to use the shelf to reach
Camper Bay, however, so you must regain the trail at the second access
trail you meet after 150 Yard Creek. If you have stayed on the trail at
150 Yard Creek, you will likely encounter muddy conditions on the way
to Camper Bay. A boardwalk helps you over some of the rough sections, but expect to encounter wet conditions in this stretch since all

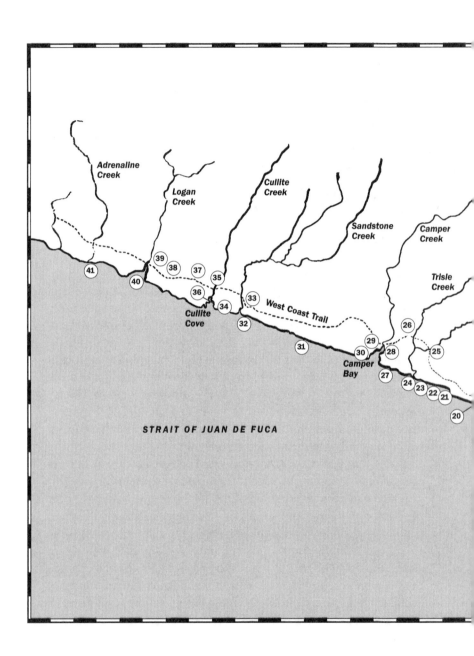

Adrenaline
Creek

Logan
Creek

Cullite
Creek

Sandstone
Creek

Camper
Creek

Trisle
Creek

West Coast Trail

Cullite
Cove

Camper
Bay

STRAIT OF JUAN DE FUCA

12

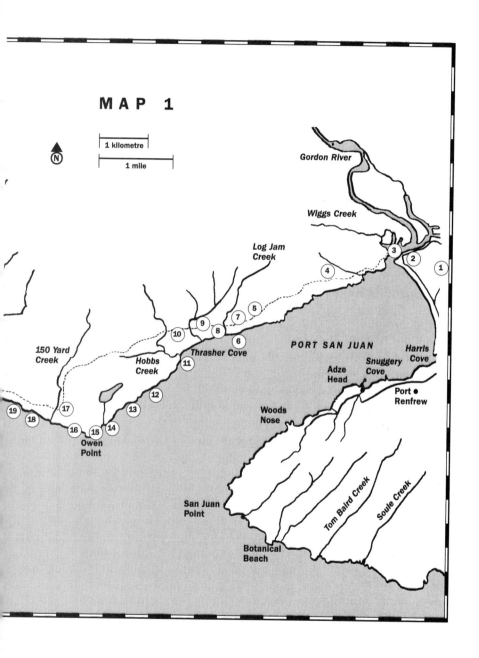

MAP 1

1 kilometre

1 mile

N

Gordon River

Wiggs Creek

Log Jam
Creek

150 Yard
Creek

Hobbs
Creek

Thrasher Cove

PORT SAN JUAN

Harris
Cove

Snuggery
Cove

Adze
Head

Port ●
Renfrew

Woods
Nose

Owen
Point

San Juan
Point

Botanical
Beach

Tom Baird Creek

Soule Creek

NOTES TO MAP 1

1   *Pacheenaht Indian Reserve.*

2   *West Coast Trail Information Centre. Permits and orientation sessions are given here. The pickup location for the ferry across the Gordon River is nearby.*

3   *Beginning of West Coast Trail.*

4   *It is easy to lose the trail in this area because of the dense vegetation.*

5   *Old donkey engine left over from former logging.*

6   *Steep gravel slope just below trail. Beach access in an emergency; however, slope is dangerous.*

7   *High point on the trail. Small campsite with water at nearby creek. Between [5] and [7] the trail passes through open areas with good views of Port San Juan.*

8   *Log Jam Creek. Trail steep on both sides of the creek.*

9   *Pleasant rest stop. Possible campsite.*

10   *Intersection of trail to Thrasher Cove. Trail to Thrasher is steep with ladders.*

11   *Thrasher Cove. Excellent camping on sandy beach. Water available at Hobbs Creek.*

12   *Landslide area. Use caution.*

13   *Sandstone shelf begins. Beach hiking at low tide only. Relatively fast west of here, slower to the east.*

14   *Cleft Falls. Interesting sea caves to the west of here.*

15   *Owen Point. Possible to walk around if tide is below 1.8 metres (6 feet). A bypass trail exists over the point. Possible campsite in an emergency. Area to the west is known as Moonscape because of unusual eroded sandstone.*

16   *Surge channels break the shelf in this area. Use caution.*

17   *150 Yard Creek. Good, small campsite. Pool and cavern below campsite.*

18   *First beach access trail.*

19   *Second beach access trail.*

20   *Shelf from here to [24] is impassable at high tide.*

21 Small shady cove.

22 Last beach access trail before Trisle Creek.

23 Impassable.

24 Sandstone shelf ends in deep, wide channel. Good camping at mouth of Trisle Creek.

25 Small campsite on creek.

26 Blowdown area. Follow route over logs.

27 Impassable—Trinity Caves.

28 Camper Creek. Cable car crossing. Creek is dangerous in high water.

29 Camper Bay. Excellent campsite. Outhouse. Quu'as guardian cabin. Beach access from Camper Bay is potentially hazardous, especially at high tides.

30 Sandstone shelf is broken by channel that is impassable at high tide. If it is passable, the rest of the route to Sandstone Creek will also be passable unless you have a rapidly incoming tide.

31 Surge channels—use caution.

32 Sandstone shelf ends at Sandstone Creek. It is very difficult to climb onto this shelf if heading south to Port Renfrew. Access up the creek to the trail.

33 Sandstone Creek bridge. Good rest stop but no camping.

34 No access for hikers along this portion of the sandstone shelf.

35 Cullite Creek—cable car crossing.

36 Cullite Cove—beautiful campsite; unreachable when creek is high.

37 Bog, with no forest cover. Stay on the boardwalk. Botanically interesting.

38 End of boardwalk.

39 Logan Creek. Suspension bridge.

40 Good campsite at Logan Creek. It is possible to walk along the beach route most of the way from here to the Cheewhat River when the tide is low.

41 Adrenaline Creek surge channel. Strongly advise against attempting to cross. Very slippery. Passable at low tides (1.2 metres, or 4 feet) in dry weather and with calm seas. Waterfall is a problem in the early season.

the mountain runoff collects here. This is the time that you will be looking forward to putting on the dry socks in your pack.

Between Trisle Creek and Camper Bay you will pass through a blow-down area. Such areas will become more common if the government permits logging companies to operate less than a kilometre (0.6 mile) from the shore boundary. The trees along the coastal forest protect each other from such blowdowns through wind pruning; because the trees grow evenly, strong ocean winds pass overhead instead of swirling into open spaces. A good example of this pruning can be seen from the tidal marker at the beginning of the trail. A wedge of salal growing from the first trees right down to the beach has created a protective belt.

There are ladders to be negotiated at Camper Creek. A cable car enables you to get across the creek in high water. If the creek is low, you can wade across; but if you are worried about your ability or the possible danger of high water, you should use the cable car, since Camper Creek can be dangerous to cross. Generally, wading across streams you encounter along the trail is quicker and easier, given the right conditions.

Cable cars require a certain technique to operate them. To begin with, each cable car is limited to two individuals. One person should hold the car steady, while the other one loads the packs in the middle

∧ Between 150 Yard Creek and Camper Creek, West Coast Trail. BO MARTIN
< Hiking the West Coast Trail near Thrasher Cove. BO MARTIN

of the car and then gets in the car at one end. The sitting person can then hold the car steady while the other person climbs aboard. When all is ready, let go of the line and the car will usually skim quickly along to the middle of the cable. Be careful not to bounce the car or it may disengage from the cable. After you reach the midpoint, the real work begins. Both passengers must exert effort to haul the car to the opposite shore. This task can be quite tedious and tiring, especially on longer cable car crossings. Other cautionary notes: take care not to get your fingers jammed in the pulleys. A good pair of gloves comes in handy in pulling yourself across. If you are travelling in a large group, it is much easier for the members of the group stationed on the platform to haul the car across than it is for the passengers to do so.

Camper Bay is a good campsite. Like other good sites, however, it tends to become overcrowded during peak season (June to August). It bears repeating that you are in a wilderness area and are directly responsible for the disposal of the waste you create. The cabin at Camper Bay is for the Native trail guardians with the Quu'as program. Do not bother them unless you have an emergency or wish to report a major maintenance problem that you have encountered on the trail.

Between Camper Bay and Sandstone Creek you have a choice of hiking either along the beach or on the trail. The beach route is easier to hike but is only passable when the tide is very low, below 1.2 metres (4 feet). At medium tides the shelf will be covered, and even at low tide you may have to wade off the shelf at Sandstone Creek. To regain the main trail at Sandstone go up the right side of the waterfall using the fixed wire cable. This route is passable only when the stream levels are low, in midsummer. You may have to hike in the stream in several spots. If you are hiking in the opposite direction, look for the beach access trail before you cross the bridge over Sandstone Creek. Hikers going from north to south may have difficulty in climbing onto the shelf at the mouth of Sandstone Creek while carrying a pack. If you are inexperienced or doubtful about the tide, it is probably best to stay on the trail. If you do elect to hike the trail from Camper Bay, you must first climb the ladders behind the campsite. From the top of the ladders, it is fairly routine slogging to the ladders at Sandstone Creek. The trail from Sandstone to Cullite Creek is relatively easy and can be done quickly. Cullite Cove offers a beautiful campsite on the southeast side of the creek, but the creek gully is usually so wet that it is difficult to

Near Camper Creek, West Coast Trail. ADRIAN DORST

maintain a cooking fire. In such cases, a small gas stove is worth the weight in your pack. To reach the campsite, do not cross the creek on the cable car but proceed downstream on the east side. The original access trail to the campsite was eliminated in a landslide, so the going may be a bit rough in parts.

The trail from Cullite to Logan Creek goes through a large bog. You should stay on the boardwalk, not only to save yourself from taking a mud bath, but also to protect the fragile environment. Most of the plants here are fighting for their survival in the high-acid, low-nitrogen ecosystem.

Once across the bog you face a steep descent by ladders to Logan Creek, which is spanned by an attractive suspension bridge. If you are travelling in a large group, note the precaution that only six people at a time should be on the bridge.

There is good camping at Logan Creek; if you intend to stop here for the night or for a rest, don't cross the bridge but descend the ladders to the campsite. There is good beachcombing at Logan Creek; since it is the most southerly beach along the trail, it collects flotsam from the open ocean.

Between Logan and Walbran Creeks, you have a choice of the trail route (slow and muddy but not difficult) and the potentially dangerous beach route, which should be used only when tides are below 2 metres (6.5 feet) and the seas are calm. The tide problem is at Adrenaline Creek, where a deep surge channel runs all the way to a cliff. This channel can be crossed only if the waves are small and the tide is low enough to expose a rock in the middle. Even if this rock is exposed, it is usually slippery, so it is best to slither around the edge of the channel, preferably with the assistance of a rope. The crossing is further complicated by Adrenaline Creek, which enters the scene as a waterfall and makes all of the rocks slippery. Inexperienced hikers should not attempt this crossing. It should not be attempted in the early season (May–June), when the water in Adrenaline Creek is high, since the waterfall tends to prevent the crossing. The PRNP strongly recommends against trying this route. In recent years a number of accidents, including a fatality, have occurred here. A few other surge channels in the area may also present some difficulties.

Walbran Creek is usually crossed via the cable car, but expect a long haul. If you have hiked along the trail, you will descend to the creek on a series of ladders. There is an excellent swimming hole in the creek, but remember to use no soap or only the biodegradable kind if you must bathe. Walbran Creek is named after Captain John T. Walbran, the author of *British Columbia Coast Names.*

The Walbran marks the end (or the beginning for hikers travelling in the opposite direction) of the difficult hiking. Many groups camp here, and there is a good campsite in the trees on the Port Renfrew side of the creek.

From the Walbran it is only a few hundred metres to a long, sandy beach that is reachable from the creek when the tide is low. Hiking from here to Carmanah along the beach looks easy enough, but the sand is so fine that you must learn a new style of walking. After a while you will discover through experience where the sand is hardest. Try the water's edge or the high-tide mark, where the sand is darker. When the tide is out, the rock shelf provides good hiking. A bypass trail has been built around Vancouver Point, which could be an obstacle at high tide. If you get tired of hiking the beach, there is a good trail from Walbran Creek to Vancouver Point.

Hiking on the beach is the recommended route from Kulaht Creek to Bonilla Creek. A good campsite is found at Bonilla Creek just before Bonilla Point. The point itself is marked by a large triangle that corresponds to the one across the Strait of Juan de Fuca at Cape Flattery; these signs mark the official designation of the strait as internal waters, as opposed to the open ocean. *Bonilla* means "high" in Spanish. Originally Bonilla Point was assigned as a name for Carmanah Point, where the lighthouse stands atop the cliff. By mistake the name was given to the present point, which is low and belies its Spanish name.

There is a good campsite at Bonilla Creek and an excellent waterfall nearby if you are in the mood for a shower.

Carmanah Creek may be crossed by wading or by using the cable car. If you wade across, use a stave or poles for balance. You should not try to wade across this creek in high water or on an incoming tide. There is good camping around Carmanah Creek, but many other parts of that wide, sweeping beach are clogged with driftwood. At the Bamfield end of the beach on the Indian reserve, there is a small settlement. Over the last few years the Nytom family has operated a small restaurant and food store here. The beer is cold and the conversation as spicy as the food.

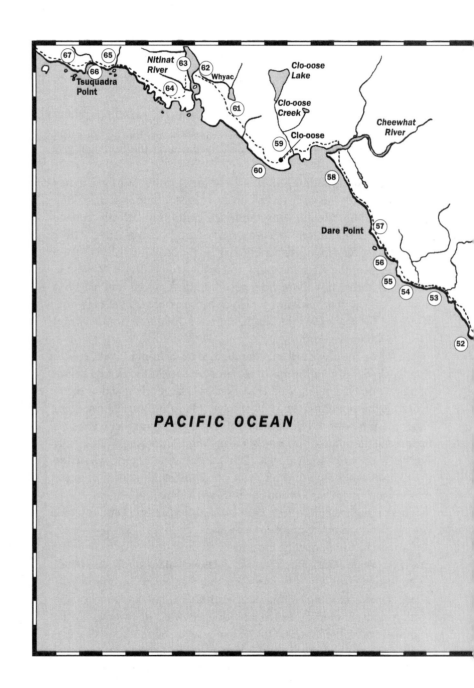

PACIFIC OCEAN

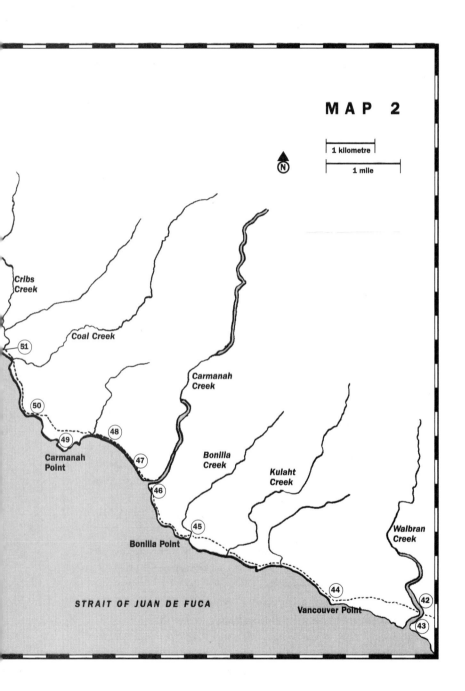

MAP 2

1 kilometre

1 mile

N

Cribs
Creek

Coal Creek

51

Carmanah
Creek

50

48

49

47

Carmanah
Point

Bonilla
Creek

46

Kulaht
Creek

45

Walbran
Creek

Bonilla Point

44

Vancouver Point

42

43

STRAIT OF JUAN DE FUCA

23

NOTES TO MAP 2

42 *Walbran Creek—cable car crossing.*

43 *Walbran Creek campsite. Excellent camping. Beach route from here to Carmanah Point is passable at high tide but best at low tide.*

44 *Vancouver Point. It may be necessary to take the bypass route around this point at high tide.*

45 *Bonilla Point. Good camping at Bonilla Creek. Waterfall. Bonilla Point is marked by a large triangular navigational aid, which corresponds to the one at Cape Flattery on the Olympic Peninsula. Officially marks the transition between the Pacific Ocean and the Strait of Juan de Fuca.*

46 *Carmanah Creek—cable car crossing.*

47 *Carmanah Creek. Good campsite on lighthouse side of the creek.*

48 *Indian reserve. Residence of the Nytom family.*

49 *Carmanah Point lighthouse. Trail passes behind it.*

50 *Beach access trail. It is possible to hike the beach around Carmanah Point at low tide, but the route is rocky and slippery.*

51 *Cribs Creek. Good campsite.*

52 *Prominent headland. Beach route from here to [57] is passable at low tide, but trail route is easier.*

53 *Beach access trail.*

54 *Wreckage of the Santa Rita may be visible in a surge channel at low tide.*

55 *Surge channel and ledge block the beach route. Rough bypass trail. Use caution.*

56 *Beach access trail up steep ladders.*

57 *Dare Point. Good camping to the west of here. Drinking water may be scarce.*

58 *Trail leaves beach and crosses peninsula to Cheewhat River suspension bridge.*

59 *Intersection with Brown's Bay Trail, which is in poor condition. Stay on the trail that is within Indian reserve.*

60 *No beach access. Anchor of Skagit, wrecked in 1906, on shelf to left, is visible from viewpoint.*

61 *Indian reserve land. Remain on trail and boardwalk through this area.*

62 *Nitinat Narrows ferry crossing. Charge for crossing here is usually $ 7 per person. Often possible to purchase fish or crabs here.*

63 *Trail resumes on far side of Nitinat Narrows. Take trail to your left.*

64 *Trail passes through rocky bluffs, affording good views.*

65 *Indian reserve. No camping on the beach. Area is patrolled by Native guardians.*

66 *Tsuquadra Creek. Site of Quu'as cabin.*

67 *Impassable headlands.*

At the end of Carmanah Beach, you will spy a trail opening between some alder that leads to a ladder. The trail climbs over the headland behind Carmanah lighthouse and through the forest to the next beach. The lighthouse has been here since 1891. It is possible to hike around Carmanah Point at low tide, but expect to do a fair amount of scrambling on slippery rocks. The section from Carmanah Point to Klanawa River is, in the opinion of many hikers, the most scenic part of the trail. Not only does the terrain alternate between forest and coastline, but the cliffs are less continuous, offering more opportunity for beach exploration.

At the Bay of the Cribs, the hiking is easy by either beach or forest. At the south end of the bay there is a prominent headland, which is visible almost to Nitinat Narrows. It is possible to continue along the shelves from here to Dare Point but only at low tide. There is a surge channel along the way that may be difficult to negotiate. If the tide is too high, you can use the access trails and ladders located both before and after this chasm. The trail from the Cribs rises steeply and traverses the top of the cliff almost to Dare Point, where it drops to sea level. After descending the long flight of stairs above the beach, hikers may regain the beach near Dare at the end of the boardwalk. A campsite with water is located at the south end of the sandy beach.

From Dare to the Cheewhat River the trail goes over old sand dunes that have been colonized by forest. There are lots of flat, sheltered campsites along the trail, as well as camping spots along the beach. Drinking water can be a problem to find; the nearest places to fill your water bottles are the north side of the Cheewhat Bridge and the south end of the sandy beach.

The Cheewhat is a slow-flowing tidal river called "river of urine" by the Ditidaht because of its colour and bad taste. Better drinking water is available from a small creek at the north end of the bridge. The bridge across the Cheewhat was built in 1976 and is a favourite subject of photographers. If you are hiking to Port Renfrew, keep to the right after crossing the bridge. Cheewhat Lake is located approximately 5 kilometres (3 miles) north of this spot but is not reachable by trail. The lake is a wintering ground for rare trumpeter swans.

The area around Clo-oose has many signs of past settlement. Clo-oose has been a Native settlement for many years. White settlers began to arrive in the 1880s, when William Grove obtained an acre of

Campsite near Cheewhat, West Coast Trail. ADRIAN DORST

land before the boundaries of the Indian reserve were established in 1892. In the 1890s William Stone arrived as the first missionary in the area, and the Logan family came to homestead. In 1912, land was developed, and several dozen white people settled in the area, mainly to the east and west of Clo-oose. Clo-oose residents, along with the lighthouse keepers and the linemen, often played heroic roles in the rescue of shipwrecked mariners. This small community contributed a disproportionate share of young men in World War I, and after the war the community declined. Other factors were isolation, the closing of the fish cannery on Nitinat Lake, the decline of the salmon fishery and, in the 1950s, the withdrawal of the coastal steamer *Maquinna* as many west coast communities became accessible by road or float plane. The last of the original white families left in 1952. With the creation of the national park, the private land holdings were all expropriated and transferred to the federal government.

Hikers are required by the Ditidaht Band to remain on the trail through the Clo-oose area. Quu'as guardians patrol the trail and all reserve lands, which are off-limits for camping and exploring. All such lands are well marked with signs advising hikers that there is no trespassing or camping on reserve land.

From Clo-oose, the trail climbs to the top of a cliff, where there are spectacular views, especially at sunset. Watch your footing here, since the drop-off is quite steep. It is not possible to hike along the shore all the way from Clo-oose to Whyac. Whyac is a very old village, possibly one of the oldest on the west coast of North America. When the first white explorer, Dr. Robert Brown, travelled to this area in 1864, Whyac was the principal village of the Ditidaht people. It was strongly fortified and considered to be impregnable by the inhabitants. Dr. Brown described the Ditidaht as having "a high reputation as hunters, whale fishers, and warriors."

The trail bypasses Whyac, and you must remain on the trail and not visit the village. In the past hikers have been responsible for vandalizing and destroying many sacred sites of the First Nations people.

At Nitinat Narrows there is a ferry service to take you across, for $7 per person at the time of this publication. The current operator of the ferry service is Carl Edgar, who has ferried hikers across the narrows for over twenty years. For a higher fee ($25 at time of this edition), he will take you by boat to the Ditidaht village at the eastern end of Nitinat Lake. This same service is offered to hikers who join the trail at Nitinat Lake. There is a trail information centre at the head of the lake where permits are issued and orientation sessions are conducted. Further information is given in Chapter 6.

Nitinat Narrows is one of the most spectacular locations on the entire west coast of Vancouver Island and one of the most dangerous. Tidal currents roar through at speeds up to 8 knots, creating treacherous whirlpools. The outgoing tide is particularly dangerous—as it meets incoming ocean swells, huge standing waves are formed. The only really safe time for taking a small boat through the narrows is at

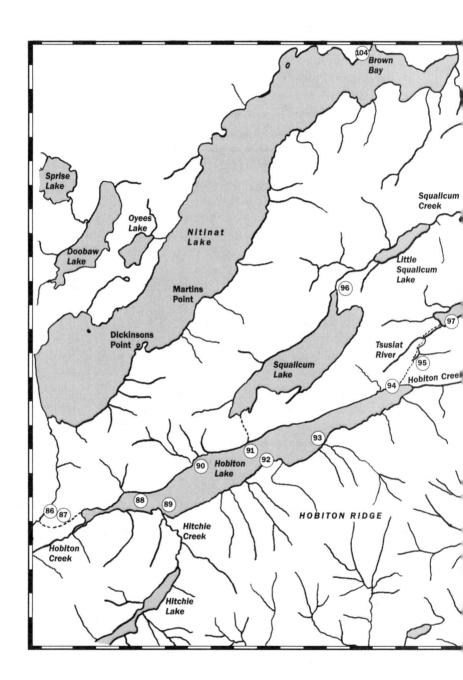

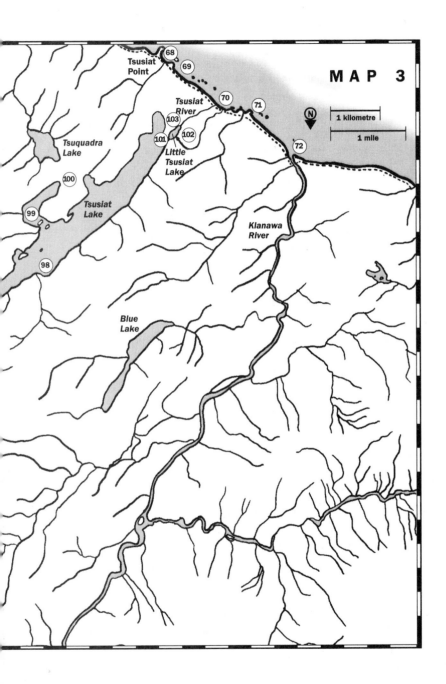

MAP 3

Tsusiat Point

68
69

Tsusiat River

70
71

103
102
101

Little Tsusiat Lake

Tsuquadra Lake

100

72

99

Tsusiat Lake

98

Klanawa River

Blue Lake

N

1 kilometre

1 mile

NOTES TO MAP 3

68 *Tsusiat Point. Impassable at high tide—use bypass trail.*

69 *Trail over headland. From here to Tsusiat Falls easily passable at low tide.*

70 *Tsusiat Falls. Excellent campsite but tends to be crowded. Outhouse located up ladders to the east of the falls.*

71 *Impassable headland.*

72 *Klanawa River. Cable car crossing. Good campsite along beach, but watch the incoming tides.*

86 *Start of portage trail to Hobiton Lake is in cove to west of point with triangular marker.*

87 *Portage trail is rough in areas. Allow about an hour to carry a canoe to Hobiton Lake.*

88 *Dead Alder campsite. Room for several tents when water level is low.*

89 *Hitchie Creek campsite.*

90 *Good campsite.*

91 *Portage trail to Squalicum Lake is steep and rough. Start of trail is marked by tape.*

92 *Good campsite.*

93 *Cedar Log campsite.*

94 *Start of portage trail to Tsusiat Lake, marked by tape. Portage is rough because of mud and deadfall.*

95 *Bypass trail around sphagnum bog.*

96 *Logjam.*

97 *Limited campsite is wet and boggy.*

98 *Good campsite.*

99 *Lagoon; crab apple trees around perimeter.*

100 *Old trail.*

101 *Good campsite. Logjam marks creek entrance. Carry canoes over logjam.*

102 *Little Tsusiat Lake—lots of water lilies.*

103 *Portage trails on either side of creek.*

104 *Brown Bay. Access to West Coast Trail from Nitinat Lake. Trail is in poor condition and starts from the left side of the bay next to old shack.*

---

high-water slack, a period of six minutes each day. Many drownings have occurred here. Do not try to swim across this channel, even if you are stranded and waiting for a ferry to arrive.

The portion of the trail between Nitinat Narrows and the Klanawa River is considered by many to be the most dramatically beautiful part of the West Coast Trail. It has almost everything: sweeping sandy beaches, sea caves, rocky headlands, shelves teeming with marine life and the famous Tsusiat Falls. It can be hiked in a long day but deserves a more leisurely visit.

From the narrows the trail climbs again, and you get glimpses of the sea as it surges against headlands and chasms. Between here and Tsusiat Falls there are many camping areas, but water can be a problem during the dry season. The trail rejoins the beach about 1.5 kilometres (about 1 mile) from Nitinat, and from this point to Tsusiat Falls you can do most of your hiking along the beach. You will have to leave the beach route to get around the headlands at Tsuquadra Point and Tsusiat Point, and certain other parts are passable only if the tide is right. There is no trespassing at the Tsuquadra Indian reserve. This area is patrolled by Quu'as guardians, who are stationed at a cabin near Tsuquadra Creek.

Tsusiat Falls has become a popular gathering place; during the height of the season, many groups will be camped here. Consequently, litter and sanitation are problems. In particular, the shallow sea caves in the Tsusiat area should not be used as latrines. You should carry a small trowel or other digging tool in order to properly dispose of your waste in the forest floor. The outhouses are located up the ladders to the east of the falls. If you don't want to take the long trip up to visit them, then use the intertidal flush system to dispose of your waste. This means choosing a spot where the high tide is likely to flush your waste out to sea. If you do decide to climb up the ladders to use the facilities, the outhouses should not be used for the disposal of garbage. It is hoped that the PRNP will recognize that the outhouses should be relocated in a more convenient spot. In addition, the use of non-biodegradable soap is causing a problem with algal growth in the pool below the falls. Drinking water should be obtained from the falls and not the pool.

Tsusiat Falls is also a junction of the Hobiton–Tsusiat canoeing circuit, which is described in Chapter 3. There are rough portage trails up both sides of Tsusiat Creek to Tsusiat Lake.

From Tsusiat Falls to the Klanawa River, you are completely separated from the ocean except for one or two rough and steep access points. The cable car ride across the Klanawa is an exciting experience, but if you are alone, the journey will be hard on your shoulders. It is best if one person rides in the car and pulls while a partner assists

31

from shore. The Klanawa, like the Cheewhat, is tidal, so you may have to go a fair way upstream to obtain potable water. You should also keep the tide in mind when selecting your picturesque campsite on the banks of the river.

It is possible to hike from the Klanawa to the trail's end in one day, but it is a long hike and the scenery deserves to be enjoyed. Water is plentiful, with the possible exception of the low portion for the first 4 kilometres (2.5 miles) west of the Klanawa River. The trail proceeds mainly through the forest, but there are various spots where the beach is accessible for extended walking. You can trek from the Klanawa to Michigan Creek on the beach, except for the section between Trestle Creek and Tsocowis Creek.

The famous *Valencia* wreck of 1906 occurred near Shelter Bight, about 4 kilometres (2.5 miles) west of the mouth of the Klanawa River. An overview of the wreck site appears where the trail skirts the cliffs through an old burn, just west of a donkey engine that was left by trail builders in 1909. Over the years, the *Valencia* has sunk completely, and no remnants of wreckage are visible.

The capstan on the rocks at Shelter Bight may have come from the four-masted steam schooner *Robert E. Lewers*, which went aground in 1923. In 1895, the magnificent iron square-rigger *Janet Cowan* was wrecked, and its remains are still visible in a surge channel at the outlet of Billy Goat Creek. Finally, at the mouth of Michigan Creek lie the boiler and some smaller parts of the steam schooner *Michigan*, wrecked in 1893.

The Darling River can be forded by wading, and the crossing should pose little difficulty under normal runoff conditions. At the mouth of the Darling River are the remains of the *Uzbekistan*, a Russian steamship that went down in 1943 while carrying war materials from the west coast.

The campsites at Darling River, being fairly close to Pachena, are heavily used and susceptible to damage. Hikers are urged to treat the area gently and in particular to build fires only on the beach. Additional camping can be found near Tsocowis Creek and Michigan Creek. An especially good campsite replete with small but dry caves is located near Orange Juice Creek, the small creek to the east of the Darling River.

From Michigan Creek the trail climbs up through the forest to the Pachena lighthouse. At time of this edition, the lighthouse at Pachena

Tsusiat Falls, West Coast Trail. ADRIAN DORST

Point is staffed and drinking water is available on the grounds. It is expected that in 1998 the lighthouse at Pachena Point will be converted to a completely automatic system without any staff.

The trail from Pachena Point to the trailhead is almost a road; for many years it was the supply road for the lighthouse. The many gullies make it harder to hike than one would expect, and the trail itself is almost entirely in the forest with few viewpoints. You may want to try one or more of the several water access or view paths. In fall and early spring, sea lions can be spotted on Flat Rocks. The camping areas on the beaches below the trail have ample water.

Just past the trail's end is an Information Centre staffed by the PRNP. The centre is open from 9:00 A.M. to 5:00 P.M. daily from May 1 until October 1. You must pick up or drop off your West Coast Trail permit at the Information Centre. As an added inducement to get you to drop off your permit, Parks Canada staff will present you with a certificate stating that you have completed the hike. Day hikers do not require a permit. For further details on the permit system, see Chapter 6.

To reach Bamfield, you must go through the parking lot to the main road. Bamfield has accommodations and supplies and is also the terminus for the Bamfield–Port Alberni ferry, the *Lady Rose.*

If you want to camp at Pachena Bay, note that most of the beach

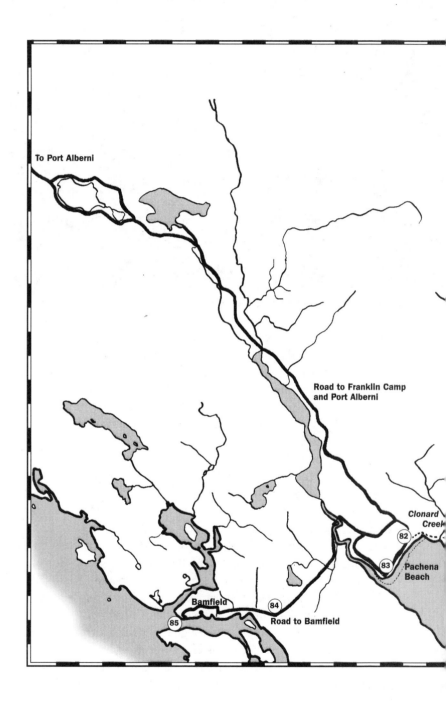

To Port Alberni

Road to Franklin Camp
and Port Alberni

Clonard
Creek

Pachena
Beach

Bamfield

Road to Bamfield

82

83

84

85

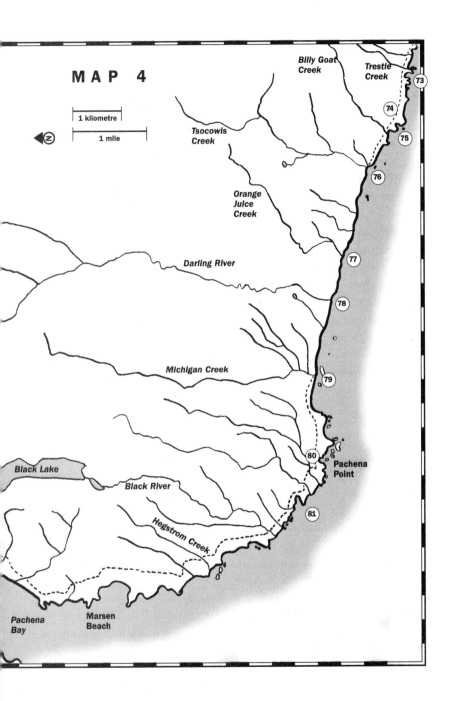

MAP 4

1 kilometre

1 mile

N

Billy Goat Creek

Trestle Creek

73

74

75

76

Tsocowis Creek

Orange Juice Creek

Darling River

77

78

79

Michigan Creek

80

Pachena Point

81

Black Lake

Black River

Hegstrom Creek

Pachena Bay

Marsen Beach

NOTES TO MAP 4

73 *Shelter Bight. It is not possible to hike along the beach route from Trestle Creek to [76]. Just west of here is the site of the Valencia grounding and wreck.*

74 *Old donkey engine.*

75 *Wreckage of the Janet Cowan may be visible in a surge channel at the mouth of Billy Goat Creek at low tide.*

76 *Trail rejoins beach route by a stream. Interesting gorge about 1 kilometre (0.6 mile) upstream.*

77 *Orange Juice Creek. Good camping*

78 *Darling River. Usually easily waded. Good campsite. No trail exists between here and Michigan Creek, so you must hike the beach route.*

79 *Michigan Creek. Good campsite. Wreckage of Michigan, 1893.*

80 *Pachena Point lighthouse. Outhouses located 100 metres (300 feet) east of lighthouse entrance along trail.*

81 *Flat Rocks sea lion colony from March to May, occasionally at other times.*

82 *End of West Coast Trail. Information Centre. Sign out and receive certificate. Camping is permitted on the beach adjacent to the grassy field for a maximum stay of three days. Outhouses located near parking lot.*

83 *Huu-Ay-Aht reserve. Commercial campground along the beach at Pachena.*

84 *Road to Bamfield. A walking trail parallels the road.*

85 *Bamfield government dock. Bamfield is terminus for Lady Rose ferry to Port Alberni and pickup location for shuttle bus services. Juan de Fuca express leaves from government dock.*

area lies within a reserve. The Huu-Ay-Aht First Nation, which owns the reserve, operates a commercial campground. Camping is also permitted on the beach near the end of the trail for a maximum stay of three nights. Camping is not permitted on the grassy area.

HIKING AROUND BAMFIELD

If you have to wait in Bamfield a day or two for transportation out or are simply exploring the area, there are a few day hikes and short excursions worth taking. A visit to the original townsite of Bamfield on the west side of Bamfield Inlet is recommended. Getting across the inlet should not be much of a problem, since water taxis regularly go back and forth. Just ask at the main dock.

The original townsite of Bamfield is much more interesting than the east side. Very few cars are seen here, and a maze of walking trails

Tsusiat Falls, West Coast Trail. ADRIAN DORST

connects with the "main street"—a boardwalk along the waterfront. Short jaunts can be made to Brady Beach and other beaches beyond by following the occasional sign.

Hiking to Cape Beale starts at a well-marked trailhead at the end of Imperial Eagle Road, where there is a small parking lot. To reach Cape Beale, proceed along the trail in a southerly direction until you reach Kicha Lake. At the junction take the right branch west to Topaltos Bay. When you reach Topaltos Bay, hike along the beach for about two-thirds of its length to a point where the trail enters the forest. The rest of the trail can be difficult as a result of mud and broken boardwalks. If your goal is the Cape Beale lighthouse, you must reach the final channel at low tide, which is the only time when it is dry. There is no camping at the lighthouse, so don't get stranded by the incoming tide.

Another interesting side trip takes you to Keeha Bay. At the Y-junction at the northern tip of Kicha Lake, take the trail to your left, which traverses the east side of the lake. The trail is in rough condition towards the southern end of the lake; you may have to bushwhack or slog through the mud to reach dry, high ground. Cape Beale or Pachena Bay may be reached from Keeha Bay, but you have to scramble over rocks, do some gruelling bushwhacking and wait for low tides in certain stretches to get around otherwise impassable headlands.

CHAPTER THREE

Canoeing the Nitinat Triangle

I F YOU WISH TO ESCAPE FROM the numbers of hikers on the West
Coast Trail and are an experienced canoeist, Nitinat Lake Triangle
offers a wilderness adventure worth attempting.

An exploratory trip from Nitinat Lake to Hobiton Lake and beyond
to Tsusiat Lake is not difficult. Completing the circuit by launching
your canoe into the surf at Tsusiat Lake and running the Nitinat
Narrows, however, is for highly experienced canoeists only.

Permits are required for those who wish to either hike or canoe in
the Nitinat Lake area. The Information Centre at the Ditidaht village at
the head of Nitinat Lake is the most convenient spot to pick these up,
although any Information Centre will issue them. The best launching
area to Nitinat Lake is from Knob Point picnic site on the north side of
Nitinat Lake. More details about access are given in Chapter 6.

A word of warning about Nitinat Lake is appropriate. First, the high
winds on the lake can be dangerous; second, it is a tidal lake and therefore
salty. A westerly wind generally sets in about ten o'clock each morning or
earlier, and the water builds into a steep chop. To avoid paddling into this
wind, you must be prepared to set off early in the morning. If you time
your trip properly, you will have the wind behind you on your return trip.

< Tsusiat Beach, West Coast Trail. ADRIAN DORST

To find the Nitinat Lake start of the portage to Hobiton Lake, paddle to the south end of the Hobiton Indian reserve, about 300 metres (1000 feet) past the mouth of Hobiton Creek. There you will find a rock point with a large triangular marker. The portage trail commences in the cove just beyond the point. At Hobiton Creek you will have to portage your canoe to Hobiton Lake. Hobiton Creek is closed to navigation, and the Department of Fisheries prohibits the handlining of canoes, since Hobiton Creek is a sockeye-salmon-bearing stream; the lining of boats is apt to destroy spawning beds and channels.

The portage is rough. Each winter brings windfalls from the coastal storms; do not expect that the trail will be well maintained. Allow about two hours for the portage, which will involve one trip with the canoe and one with packs. In addition to windfalls, there are mud holes and slippery banks. Footwear with good traction is essential at all portages.

At the end of the portage, there is a view of the north shore of Hobiton Lake, with its majestic sweep of huge fir, cedar and hemlock trees on Hobiton Ridge. Most of the campsites on the lake are scattered along the north side. At Dead Alder ten or more tents may be stretched along the shore. Hitchie Creek site can take about eight tents, and there is room for several at Cedar Log. Firewood is scarce; you should use a stove for cooking and spare the live trees. Remember also that fish spawn in the beds of the small creeks, so avoid disturbing the gravel.

The flat at the mouth of Hitchie Creek has good camping, and the breeze off the lake restricts the number of insects. There is a spectacular waterfall partway up Hitchie Creek that a determined hiker may reach by scrambling and wading. By scrambling out of the canyon near the falls and by bushwhacking, you can attain Hitchie Lake. Because this trip is dangerous and difficult and involves the use of ropes, only experienced hikers or climbers should attempt it.

The Cedar Log campsite is at the mouth of a small creek and is marked by a huge log projecting out into the water. From this campsite, it takes about an hour to climb Hobiton Ridge through the old-growth forest. There are no trails up to the ridge, but passage is relatively easy as long as you avoid the gullies. The forest is open and carpeted with ferns.

The trail to Squalicum Lake starts at a small gravel beach on the south side of Hobiton Lake. The entrance to the trail lies below a saddle in the ridge and is marked by ribbon. Enormous mossy trees line the trail, which rises steeply 150 metres (500 feet). It is not recommended to take canoes over this trail, but if you are so inclined you should have at least two others with you to help.

Squalicum Lake is scenic, but difficult to explore without a canoe or raft. From its western end, Squalicum Creek runs westward through two small lakes to discharge into Tsusiat Lake. The descent of this creek is extremely rough. There is a 9-metre-high (30-foot-high) waterfall about 365 metres (400 yards) up from Tsusiat Lake.

The entrance to the portage between Hobiton and Tsusiat Lakes is on the south shore to the east of the end of Hobiton Lake. It is marked by a large log sloping into the lake and by tape. The portage is rough, with large deadfall, mud holes and slippery banks. You will need about two hours to carry a canoe over the trail; with a pack, the portage may take about an hour.

The portage passes beside a pretty bog on the crest of a ridge. Tiny sundews—insectivorous plants—are found in the mossy sections here. A bypass trail around this bog was constructed by volunteers from Mt. Douglas Secondary School in Victoria and members of the Sierra Club.

As you approach Tsusiat Lake on the portage, the trees become smaller. The portage ends at the east end of Tsusiat Lake. Enough space has been cleared to provide camping space for a small group, but the site is boggy and cramped. Tsusiat Lake has a very different character from that of Hobiton Lake. Although Hobiton Ridge still dominates the view, it is now much farther away. The timber along the shores is smaller, and there are islands with interesting examples of stunted growth.

If there is no wind, it will take between one and one and a half hours to paddle to the western end of the lake. Approximately halfway along the south shore, near a small island, you will spot the narrow entrance to the lagoon. The Ditidaht used this sheltered location in former times as a place of refuge when enemies were harassing them. The lagoon is shallow and usually warm—a good place for a dip. Some canoeists have reported a rather surprising nuisance on Tsusiat Lake during July and August: seagulls are often so numerous as to be bothersome.

A trail to Tsuquadra Lake leaves from the southwest tip of the lagoon, but the trail is very overgrown and quite difficult to find. Another trail leads from the lagoon up Squalicum Creek to the falls, but this trail is extremely rough.

There are not as many campsites on Tsusiat Lake as on Hobiton Lake. The good locations are on the northwest shore. Another good camping site is at the far west end near the logjam marking the out-flow from the lake.

You will probably not want to take your canoe down Tsusiat Creek. Leave it at Little Tsusiat Lake and hike down. There are trails on either side of the creek; the one on the south side is better. Do not walk in the creek, since it is fragile and exhibits signs of damage from overuse.

If you do wish to take your canoe down to the sea, go over the log-jam, move into Little Tsusiat Lake and enter Tsusiat Creek, which is quite shallow. Use the portage trails on either side of the creek.

If you are an expert canoeist, you can take your canoe down the lad-ders to the beach at Tsusiat Falls and launch your canoe through the surf. You can then paddle east to Nitinat Narrows and through to Nitinat Lake. Be warned that this journey is potentially very dangerous and should be attempted only if you are a highly experienced ocean canoeist.

If you miscalculate when launching into the surf, you will probably suffer only a soaking or the loss of your equipment. If you miscalculate when canoeing through Nitinat Narrows, you could lose your life, as have many people. It is only really safe at slack tide, preferable high-water slack, which lasts about six minutes each day.

Remember that slack water in the narrows does not occur when the ocean tide is slack but rather when the level of Nitinat Lake is equal to that of the ocean. At the high ocean tide there may be a very strong flow through the narrows and into the lake. You will need west coast tide and current tables. Read them accurately and allow for daylight saving time. Of course, the sea must be calm enough for canoeing. Especially avoid strong southwesterly winds. These give a strong following sea that can cause a canoe to run out of control and capsize. Also watch out for outly-ing shelves and the Nitinat Bar, over which swells sometimes break sud-denly. These warnings may sound melodramatic, but the ocean is not like a sheltered lake. If you are not experienced at canoeing along the open ocean, you can get into trouble very easily. Because of the strong surf and cliff-lined shoreline, you cannot simply go ashore. If you cap-size, twenty minutes in the frigid ocean is enough to cause hypothermia and loss of consciousness. To repeat: **Nitinat Narrows is extremely dan-gerous, particularly for inexperienced boaters.**

An alternative route from Tsusiat Falls to Nitinat Lake that avoids the narrows (and arguably is a bit safer) is to paddle by sea to the beach at Clo-oose, land your canoe through the surf and portage to Brown Bay on Nitinat Lake. You should seek permission of the Ditidaht before doing so, since you will be using the reserve at Clo-oose to land and the portage trail goes through their reserve. The portage trail is in rough shape and passes close to Clo-oose Lake.

If you have canoed from Tsusiat Lake and through the narrows, you should not have any problems with lake turbulence. Remember the midday winds and allow yourself time to pull ashore for a few hours if the winds become too strong. If the winds are not too strong, however, you can sail back up the lake.

In general, Hobiton Lake can by enjoyed in a weekend, but to reach and explore Tsusiat Lake takes at least three days. Allow another two days if you want to reach the sea from Tsusiat Lake.

CHAPTER FOUR

Hiking the
Juan de Fuca
Marine Trail

L IKE THE WEST COAST TRAIL, the Juan de Fuca Marine Trail had its origins in the 1889 telegraph line constructed between Victoria and Bamfield. Unlike the better-known and more popular West Coast Trail, however, the trail between Port Renfrew and Jordan River did not form part of the Life Saving Trail and thus disappeared for many decades.

As the West Coast Trail became more popular and more crowded, a number of backpackers became convinced that alternative routes should be set aside for recreational hiking. In the 1970s members of the Victoria Sierra Club began to lobby the provincial government to preserve the southern coast along the Strait of Juan de Fuca between Jordan River and Botanical Beach near Port Renfrew. At the same time *Victoria Colonist* columnist Alec Merriman began promoting the preservation of Botanical Beach and other areas along the coast. The Sierra Club launched various exploratory forays into the thick bush in an attempt to link some of the more popular beaches, such as Mystic and Sombrio. Unfortunately, logging companies began harvesting Crown land under forestry tenure in the area surrounding Sombrio Creek and Parkinson Creek. In the early 1980s, the Sierra Club

< Headland, West Coast Trail. ADRIAN DORST

launched its first civil action in a Canadian court in an attempt to fore-stall the logging. Although this legal action failed, the case was the first in a series of legal actions brought by the Sierra Club that resulted in the formation of the Sierra Legal Defence Fund in Canada to promote the use of court actions to preserve wilderness in the province.

In the meantime, as a result of the efforts of the Victoria Sierra Club, the Capital Regional District set aside the "West Coast Strip," as it was called in those days, as a planned future park. In the 1990s the provincial government saw the usefulness of preserving wilderness and recreational access to it and acquired the land base for the present Juan de Fuca Marine Trail.

The Juan de Fuca Marine Trail was set aside as a provincial park in 1995. The trail is 47 kilometres (29 miles) long and connects Botanical Beach at the west end and China Beach at the eastern terminus. It parallels Provincial Highway 14, which links Victoria and Port Renfrew. The trail affords views of the Strait of Juan de Fuca, named for the Greek pilot who explored the straight in 1592. De Fuca, who was travelling from Mexico, is believed to have sailed as far as the Strait of Georgia that year. The trail also gives access to some of the more remote beaches on the southwest coast of Vancouver Island.

Since the trail is still relatively new, it is also very much a trail in transition; parts of it are being upgraded by B.C. Parks staff, and campsites are being modified or moved. Before beginning your hike, check with provincial park rangers at B.C. Parks for up-to-date trail conditions. You should also consult tide tables, since there are many places where you must hike the beach and stretches of the coast are not accessible at high tides. Tide tables are posted by B.C. Parks at all trailheads. The tables for Sooke are good for China Beach and Mystic Beach; the Tofino tide tables are good for Bear Beach to Botanical Beach. The following table lists the locations where you may encounter a tide problem:

Kilometres from China Beach	Passable at tides below:
8.7	3 metres (10 feet)
20.6	2.75 metres (9 feet)
21.3	2.75 metres (9 feet)
28.05	3 metres (10 feet)
29.3–29.9	2.6 metres (8.5 feet)
30.15	3 metres (10 feet)

All beach access trails along the trail are marked by large orange-red fluorescent balls that are usually suspended high in trees adjacent to the access point.

Comparisons between the West Coast Trail and the Juan de Fuca Trail are perhaps inevitable. The newer trail is shorter and more accessible and can be readily joined at several locations, thus making it possible to hike the trail in segments rather than as one long trail. Signage along the trail is excellent, with kilometre markers clearly indicating distance from the trailhead at China Beach.

Although you do not need a permit to hike the trail, you do need to register for overnight camping. The fee is $6 per night for a party of four. If you fail to register and pay for your camping permit, you risk being assessed a fine of $50 by B.C. Parks staff. Campfires are permitted only below the high-water marks on the beach. B.C. Parks staff advises that a permit system may be required in the future if the trail becomes crowded and more heavily used.

The Juan de Fuca eastern trailhead is reached from Victoria by an easy drive of approximately two and a half hours. Ample parking is available at the turnoff to China Beach; park in the first parking lot. Expect the first part of the trail to be muddy except during dry spells in the summer. On weekends, the first stretch of the trail to Mystic Beach is also apt to be crowded with day hikers going to Mystic Beach. Just before the 1-kilometre marker, you will cross the well-constructed suspension bridge over Pete Wolfe Creek. The trail then heads down to the first campsite at Mystic Beach, which is reached just past the 2-kilometre point. Mystic Beach is a great place to picnic or catch a shower from the waterfall sliding over the sandstone cliff, which is to the east as you reach the beach. The black rocks to the east past the waterfall lead to San Simon Point, which cannot be reached on foot.

You must walk west along the beach for a short stretch to a well-marked beach access trail in order to rejoin the main trail. The trail between Mystic Beach and the next campsite, at Bear Beach, is confined mainly to the forest, with some ocean views along the tops of cliffs just to the west of Mystic Beach. There are numerous small streams where you may fill your water bottle or relax in the shade for a rest. All the streams have good bridges.

After you cross Ivanhoe Creek, you will begin a gradual descent to Bear Beach. The small to medium-sized rocks on the beach may be slippery if wet, making hiking there quite onerous. Numerous people have twisted their ankles on this stretch while hiking with a heavy pack. Good camping is found at Rosemond Creek and Clinch Creek, farther to the west. Clinch Creek is named for the schooner *D. L. Clinch*, which was wrecked near there in 1860. Note that there is a tide problem just to the west of Rosemond Creek. At high tides the sea reaches the base of the sandstone cliffs and cuts off the rest of the beach to the west. If you encounter tides in excess of 3 metres (10 feet), you should plan to camp at Rosemond Creek or wait there until the tide drops. Tide tables are posted at the trailheads to help you plan your hike. You should use the tables for Tofino and Sooke and interpolate between the time the tide turns at each place to get an approximate reading.

The last camping spot in the vicinity of Bear Beach is located just to the east of Ledingham Creek near the 10-kilometre marker. There are pit toilets along this beach and a good water supply from the creek.

The trail section from Bear Beach to Chin Beach is the most difficult part of the hike. There are many elevation changes as the trail crosses numerous streams in this section. All of the streams drain Jordan Ridge, which is located to the north. During the rainy season (generally the off-season, although a few days of steady rain will have the same result), you will encounter a lot of mud in this section. There are also few camping opportunities in this section until you reach Chin Beach itself. If you are really in a fix, there is a small campsite near Hoard Creek. A rough beach access trail near the bridge over this creek leads down to a small gravel beach, which floods at high tide.

You will pass by Magdalena Point and Arch Rock between the 13- and 14-kilometre markers, although the point itself is not visible from the trail. The trail stays mainly in the cedar-hemlock-Sitka spruce forest, offering glimpses of the sea now and then. After you pass the 19-kilometre marker, you will begin a gradual descent to Chin Beach. At the eastern entrance to this beach, the route along the beach is cut off by tides above 2.75 metres (9 feet). If you become trapped by an incoming tide, you can take shelter in a small cabin, complete with sun room, located near the 20-kilometre marker in the forest above the beach access trail.

Chin Beach provides several good camping locations. As you walk west down the beach you will encounter a number of beach access trails. Depending on the tide, you may walk along the beach and

Near Sombrio Point, Juan de Fuca Trail. BO MARTIN

through some interesting rocky areas until you arrive at the last access trail, which, like all access trails, is marked with bright orange fluorescent buoys. This trail curls up the west side of a small stream between the 22- and 23-kilometre signposts. If you miss this turnoff, you will reach yellow signs on the beach warning you that the beach route to Sombrio is impassable beyond that point.

Provincial parks designate the route between Chin Beach and Sombrio Beach as difficult. Once again the difficulty arises as a result of the elevation changes that you will encounter in crossing a number of small streams. The highlight of this stretch of the trail is the suspension bridge across Loss Creek. From the centre of the bridge you can view beautiful sea stacks seaward and a deep, rocky gorge in the opposite direction. After you cross this bridge the trail climbs up and turns away from the coast to join an old logging road near the 25-kilometre marker. You will travel along this route for approximately a kilometre (0.6 mile) until the trail turns seaward and heads down towards Sombrio Point.

From that point the trail hugs the coastline until you descend to east Sombrio Beach. There is good camping along this stretch of beach. At low tide you can hike west along the beach to other good campsites in the forest above the pebble beach. To rejoin the Juan de Fuca Trail, look

∧ Sombrio Beach, Juan de Fuca Trail. TIM LEADEM
> Waterfall near Minute Creek, Juan de Fuca Trail. TIM LEADEM

for it as it heads into the forest before you reach the squatter's cabin. In the past there was a small community of rough cabins and sites hewn out of the bush along the entire stretch of Sombrio Beach. The buildings that you see here now are the last vestiges of the small community that was removed in the spring of 1997. The squatter's cabin is on a private land holding.

In the summer, gray whales and the occasional pod of orca may be spotted along Sombrio Beach. In the fall the Steller's sea lion also will make its appearance along this coastline.

If you plan to stop your hike here, you will head away from the beach along a trail to a junction. The right fork leads to a large parking lot. From this lot a logging road snakes up the logged hill to connect with Highway 14. Sombrio Beach is a popular destination for day hikers, picnickers and surfers, and during the summer, especially on weekends, you will find the parking lot to be full.

The left fork of the trail at the junction leads up to the suspension bridge over the Sombrio River, located just east of the 29-kilometre marker. *Sombrio* means "shady place" in Spanish. The river was named by Lieutenant Manuel Quimper, commander of the Spanish naval sloop *Princess Royal*, while on an exploratory voyage along the Strait of Juan de Fuca in 1790.

After you cross the bridge, you will hike down to join the beach. It is possible to hike along the beach at low tide all the way to Minute Creek. At high tide there are bypass trails that you may take to get around the headlands. These are somewhat difficult to spot and were not well marked at time of publication. If you are hiking from Botanical Beach, the start of the first such bypass trail between the 30- and 31-kilometre markers is somewhat obscure. To reach it, hike a few metres up a small stream; the trail climbs up a slippery muddy slope and is signed as a bypass trail.

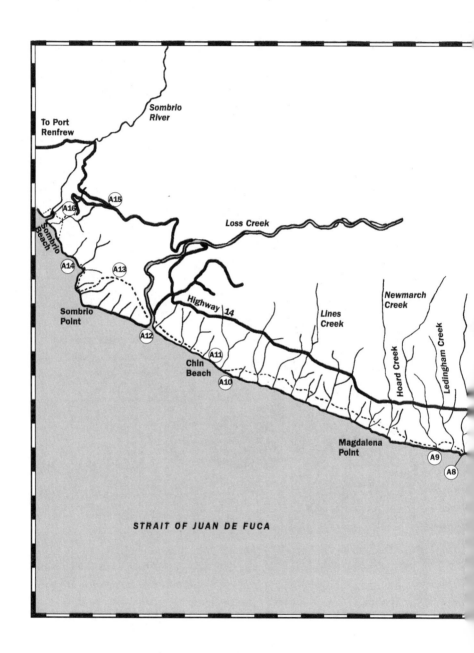

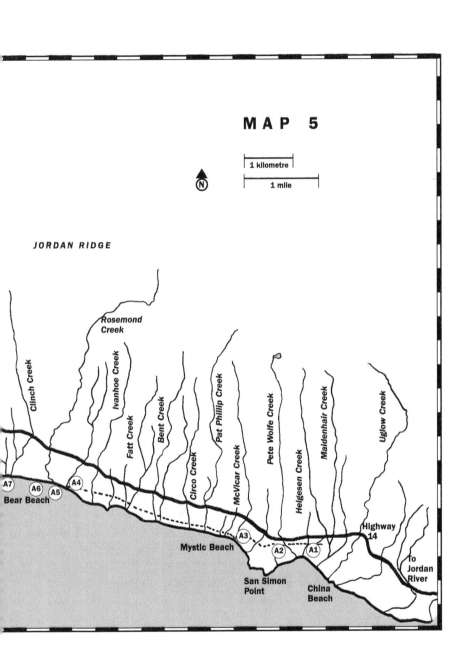

MAP 5

1 kilometre

1 mile

N

JORDAN RIDGE

Clinch Creek

Rosemond Creek

Ivanhoe Creek

Fatt Creek

Bent Creek

Pat Phillip Creek

Circo Creek

McVicar Creek

Pete Wolfe Creek

Helgesen Creek

Maidenhair Creek

Uglow Creek

A7
A6 A5
A4
Bear Beach

A3
Mystic Beach

A2

A1

Highway 14

To Jordan River

San Simon Point

China Beach

NOTES TO MAP 5

A1 *China Beach trailhead—parking lot. Bulletin board and outhouses. Start of Juan de Fuca Trail.*

A2 *Pete Wolfe Creek. Suspension bridge over gorge.*

A3 *Mystic Beach. Excellent campsite but tends to be crowded in season. Trail joins beach for short stretch before heading into forest.*

A4 *Trail rejoins beach.*

A5 *Rosemond Creek. Good campsite off beach in wooded area.*

A6 *Impassable at tides above 3 metres (10 feet). No bypass trail.*

A7 *Campsite near Clinch Creek.*

A8 *Campsite on beach before Ledingham Creek.*

A9 *Hoard Creek. Beach access and small campsite for emergency use.*

A10 *Cabin near Chin Beach. Emergency shelter. Just west of here is impassable at tides above 2.75 metres (9 feet).*

A11 *Chin Beach. Good campsites along the beach.*

A12 *Loss Creek. Suspension bridge over beautiful gorge.*

A13 *Trail follows old logging road in this area. Follow signs.*

A14 *Sombrio Beach. Camping at east Sombrio beach and west beach. Tide problem between the two beaches. Tides must be below 3 metres (10 feet) to get across. Excellent camping at both locations, though Sombrio Beach tends to be crowded.*

A15 *Trail leads up to parking lot and old logging road, which accesses Highway 14.*

A16 *Suspension bridge over Sombrio River and continuation of Juan de Fuca Trail to the west.*

Once past Sombrio, you will be in newly cut forest for approximately the next 10 kilometres (6 miles) of the trail. This logging occurred in the 1980s. The trail through the clearcut can be muddy and slippery. Watch out for the numerous salal roots that criss-cross the trail at regular intervals. In this area during the late summer and autumn you will probably see signs of black bear—usually in the form of scat festooned with salal berries. If you are hiking alone, it is a good idea to have a bear bell and to make some noise through the thick brush to warn any bear of your approach. Although B.C. Parks staff say that there is no problem with black bears in this area, it is always wise to be wary and give them plenty of warning of your arrival. You should also store your food high in a tree. More advice is given in Chapter 8.

If you have hiked the shore along the sandstone and conglomerate

View from Little Kuitshe to Sombrio Point, Juan de Fuca Trail. TIM LEADEM

shelf, you will have to rejoin the trail before Minute Creek. This creek should be crossed on the suspension bridge located upstream, since crossing on foot at its mouth at incoming tides can be quite treacherous.

Midway between kilometre markers 32 and 33 you will pass through a grassy area with access to the shelf. At high tides you will hear the rumbling of the surf in sea caves beneath the shelf. The campground at Little Kuitshe Creek is just past the 33-kilometre marker. Several tent sites have been hacked out of the salal and alder bush. A trail leads down to the coast with some good views back to Sombrio Point.

Kuitshe Creek at the 34-kilometre marker is a good stop for a rest. If you are experienced in rock scrambling, you can scramble down the left side of the waterfall downstream of the bridge and wade across the creek to reach Kuitshe Cove—a small but protected gravel beach. The trail westward from Kuitshe Creek continues through new growth until you reach the parking lot at Parkinson Creek. A rough road that is passable in a passenger car leads up for approximately 4 kilometres (2.5 miles) to connect with Highway 14. If you are accessing the trail at Parkinson Creek, the road to the parking lot is well marked off Highway 14. You will intersect several other logging roads off the main road—keep to the right as you descend to the coast to arrive at the parking lot.

The trail from the Parkinson Creek junction crosses two bridges: at the second one, which is Parkinson Creek Bridge, you will turn left to follow the creek for approximately 100 metres (300 feet). The trail then turns right, away from the logging road, to traverse through clear-cut and slash until you arrive at the coast again near kilometre marker 38. At that point, you may hike along the conglomerate shelf and explore tide pools, but watch for the orange buoys to regain the trail. After you pass kilometre marker 39 you will finally leave the clear-cut area and enter a mature cedar-hemlock forest. The going is much better here, with an abundance of boardwalks and plank walks to get you over the muddy parts.

An excellent campsite awaits you after you cross Payzant Creek at the 40-kilometre marker. Several tent platforms are set among the trees. The trail from here heads inland a bit so that you can cross Yuah Creek on a sturdy log bridge. Just past the crossing you will reach a junction with a side trail leading to Providence Cove. The cove itself is worth a visit, although B.C. Parks discourages camping there. The campsites you see in this vicinity were former ones that were abandoned for the sites at Payzant Creek.

From Providence Cove the remaining 6 kilometres (about 4 miles) of trail become progressively easier as you approach Botanical Beach. Once you cross Soule Creek on a steel-girded bridge, you will hug the west side of Soule Gorge until you reach the coast. Soule Creek takes its name from Annie Soule, who was married to Tom Baird, Jr., a son of Tom Baird, Sr., who was one of the earliest settlers in the Port Renfrew area and who donated some of the land around Botanical

∧ Conglomerate shelf, Juan de Fuca Trail. TIM LEADEM
> Near Tom Baird Creek, Juan de Fuca Trail. TIM LEADEM

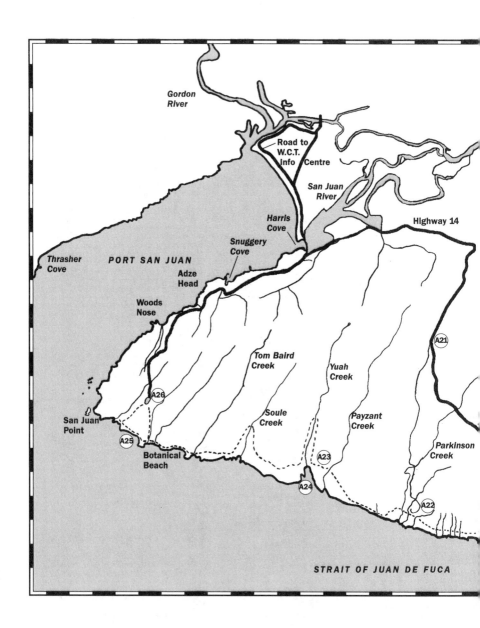

Gordon
River

Road to
W.C.T.
Info Centre

San Juan
River

Highway 14

Harris
Cove

Snuggery
Cove

Thrasher
Cove

PORT SAN JUAN

Adze
Head

Woods
Nose

Tom Baird
Creek

Yuah
Creek

A21

San Juan
Point

A26

Soule
Creek

Payzant
Creek

Parkinson
Creek

A25

Botanical
Beach

A23

A24

A22

STRAIT OF JUAN DE FUCA

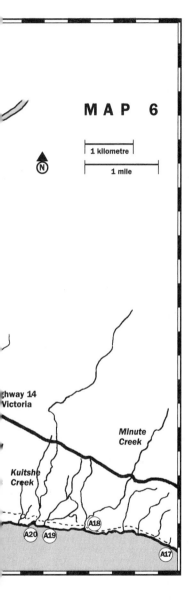

MAP 6

1 kilometre

1 mile

Highway 14
Victoria

Minute
Creek

Kuitshe
Creek

A18

A20 A19

A17

NOTES TO MAP 6

A17 *Impassable along this stretch of the coast at tides above 2.6 metres (8.5 feet). Bypass trails exist if tide is too high to hike beach route.*

A18 *Minute Creek. Suspension bridge. Creek is dangerous to wade in, in high water or on incoming tide.*

A19 *Little Kuitshe Creek campsite.*

A20 *Kuitshe Cove. Waterfall and stone beach. Difficult access.*

A21 *Parkinson Creek access road off Highway 14.*

A22 *Parking lot at Parkinson Creek. Trail follows logging road across two log bridges.*

A23 *Payzant Creek. Good campsites set among large trees.*

A24 *Providence Cove. Beautiful small cove. Good resting stop but no camping.*

A25 *Botanical Beach. Junction of trail to parking lot and access to Port Renfrew. West trail leads along shoreline to Botany Bay.*

A26 *Parking lot for Botanical Beach and end of Juan de Fuca Trail.*

Beach to the province for use as a park. From here there are a number of unmarked beach access points as you hike to the west. The last 3 kilometres (about 2 miles) before Botanical Beach are in excellent shape, with boardwalks across most of the wet sections. This section of the trail was built by youth from the T'souke and Pacheenaht First Nations. You cross Tom Baird Creek at its mouth by threading your way through a logjam—watch your footing in wet weather.

Botanical Beach is near the 46-kilometre marker. The beach is a great place for appreciating marine biology. The sandstone, conglomerate and shale rock has been eroded by the sea into many beautiful and unusual shapes, including amphitheatres, concretions and potholes in the sandstone shelf. The potholes may be observed at low tide and are a microcosm of marine life, containing anemones, coralline algae, sea urchins and starfish, to name just some of the many species of organisms that are readily spotted. This area is a special protected zone, and handling or taking of any of the wildlife is illegal. In 1901 the first marine biology station in the Pacific Northwest was built here by the University of Minnesota. Elizabeth Tilden founded the Marine Station here, and for several years the site was home to groups of biologists who studied the marine flora and fauna. Over the years the station was abandoned, and its buildings have now reverted into the thick rain forest. Many scientists, however, including a group of international botanists in 1960, have continued to assemble here to conduct studies in the biology of the area.

From Botanical Beach you may continue up an old road for approximately a kilometre (0.6 mile) to the parking lot. Or you may continue along a shoreline trail that leads to Botany Bay and an access trail to the same parking lot. The parking lot at the Botanical Beach trailhead is quite large but is apt to be crowded on the weekends.

CHAPTER FIVE

Hiking in Carmanah–Walbran Provincial Park

ARMANAH–WALBRAN PROVINCIAL PARK IS well worth visiting. Although strictly speaking the trails in this park are not coastal trails, they do afford access to some of the most beautiful old-growth forests left on the coast. Large Sitka spruce and hemlock as well as ancient western cedars line the clear, rushing waters and deep aquamarine pools of Carmanah and Walbran Creeks. Unlike the coastal trails, which resound with the omnipresent sound of crashing surf, the trails in this park will impress you with their silence.

The lower and mid-Carmanah Valley became a park in 1991. Large adjoining tracts of land in the upper Carmanah and the Walbran Creek system were added to the park by the province in 1995. The creation of this park came about after much controversy, disputes with the logging companies that controlled the tenure and mass protests followed by civil disobedience. Groups such as the Carmanah Forest Society, the Sierra Club and the Western Canada Wilderness Committee all worked to preserve this incredible forest as parkland.

At this writing B.C. Parks is discouraging hiking in the Walbran Creek portions of the park because of potentially unsafe conditions. There are no developed B.C. Parks facilities or trails in the Walbran Valley. The only area in the park with well-maintained trails is the mid-

Carmanah Valley, which is reached via Rosander Main Line. Access information for this park is found in Chapter 6. Access and trail information is also given for Walbran Creek and upper Carmanah Creek in Chapter 6. Hikers should be aware, however, that trails in the Walbran and upper Carmanah are neither maintained nor patrolled by B.C. Parks rangers. Be prepared to encounter potential dangers, and be prepared to turn back. The information listed in this guide may be inaccurate because of changing conditions along the trail. Be sure to let others know of your hiking plans, and do not take unnecessary risks. No active rescue services are available, and if you are injured, help may be a long time in coming.

TRAILS IN THE CARMANAH VALLEY

The one area of the Carmanah Park that is well maintained is near park headquarters at the end of Rosander Main Line. You will find tent platforms, drinking water and toilets here. A trail called the Valley Mist Trail leads down from the parking lot to the home of giant Sitka spruce. Since Sitka spruce has fragile, sensitive roots, you should remain on the planks and not erode the soil around the trees. After a 1.3-kilometre (1-mile) hike along the planked trail, you will reach a T-junction. To the right the Lower Carmanah Trail continues downstream to Heaven's Tree, the fallen giant and the Randy Stoltmann Commemorative Grove (formerly known as Heaven's Grove). This grove is named for the B.C. conservationist who was instrumental in convincing many people and the provincial government that this area was worth preserving from the logger's saw. A bulletin board in this area gives more information about his life. The lower trail is closed approximately 500 metres (550 yards) past this grove. The trail used to continue downstream and join the Carmanah Giant and the West Coast Trail, but the lower trail has been closed by B.C. Parks and is in unsafe condition. Access to the West Coast Trail from Carmanah–Walbran Provincial Park is not permitted.

If you turn left at the T-junction, you will hike along the Upper Carmanah Trail and encounter the Three Sisters, a group of three very tall spruce, after a hike of 1.2 kilometres (0.75 mile). No camping is permitted south of this grove. Beyond the Three Sisters, the trail becomes rougher. The first wilderness campsite, Grunt's Grove, is located about another 2 kilometres (about a mile) north of here in a grove of spruce just off the trail. There are some additional campsites along the gravel streambed during the summer, when the water levels have dropped. All of the campsites of Carmanah–Walbran are wilderness sites. Wilderness camping means no-trace camping and thus no campfires. The trail meanders away from the creek for another 2 kilometres (about a mile) and returns to the stream, where there is an excellent wilderness campsite near Paradise Pool, a deep, emerald-green pool that is perfect for bathing in hot weather.

The trail past this point is not as well maintained. You will probably encounter muddy conditions and slippery log crossings. The trail crosses the creek to the east side past Paradise Pool on a log bridge. This creek crossing may be treacherous in high water. The trail on the east side tends to be wet for the first few kilometres. After a hike of a kilometre (0.6 mile) you will reach Mystic's Hollow Camp on a wide gravel bench beside Carmanah Creek. The large tributary, which enters Carmanah Creek just north of here, is August Creek. The creek crossing at August Creek can also be difficult to negotiate over a log-jam. Just past August Creek you will reach another campsite. A side trail branches east of here to a waterfall on August Creek. Access to the Walbran Valley is along this route and is described below.

The Upper Carmanah Trail continues along the east side of Carmanah Creek for another 7.5 kilometres (4.5 miles) to the Headwaters trailhead. Here you will encounter rougher going than in the mid-Carmanah but also substantially fewer hikers. After August Creek the upper trail ascends to benchland away from the creek for the next few kilometers. The path then descends to a good campsite at Sleepy Hollow beside Maxine Creek, a clear tributary of the Carmanah. As the trail traverses the sloping sidehills, it crosses a blowdown area of wind-fallen hemlock. After the blowdown, the path rejoins the creek, where there is a beautiful box canyon followed by pools and cascades. Camp Patience is just beyond this point. Headwaters trailhead is only 3.3 kilometres (2 miles) from here. The trail ascends to another series of loud waterfalls that resound through the quiet forest. Between these waterfalls and the next campsite at Bear Paw there are a number of research projects on the insect life of the mature rain forest. Do not disturb any of the tents; they are insect traps. Entomologists have discovered thousands of new species of insects in the canopy of the forest. Most of the research is being sponsored by Forest Renewal BC. For many years the

Western Canada Wilderness Committee (wcwc) conducted research into the canopy life in this area; the organization discovered several marbled murrelet nests here. The wcwc also operated a research camp called Hummingbird Camp in a flat area beside the creek about half a kilometre (a third of a mile) before the end of the upper trail. According to B.C. Parks, this camp will be dismantled in the near future. If you plan to hike to the Headwaters trailhead, you will cross over to the west side of the creek along a bridge over a small gorge. Just before the bridge is a planked trail with the names of some of the trail builders carved into the planks. All hikers owe a debt of gratitude to the wcwc for building most of the Upper Carmanah Trail. From the bridge a trail meanders through the brush to join the spur logging road that leads to Carmanah Main Line. For further instructions on finding this trailhead by car, see Chapter 6.

If you are an experienced backpacker, you may want to hike from Carmanah Creek to West Walbran Creek. There is a very rough trail that leaves the Carmanah Creek Trail at August Creek and ascends east alongside the creek for about 2 kilometres (about a mile) before it

∧ Waterfall, Upper Carmanah Trail. TIM LEADEM
> Bridge over Upper Carmanah Trail, Headwaters trailhead. TIM LEADEM

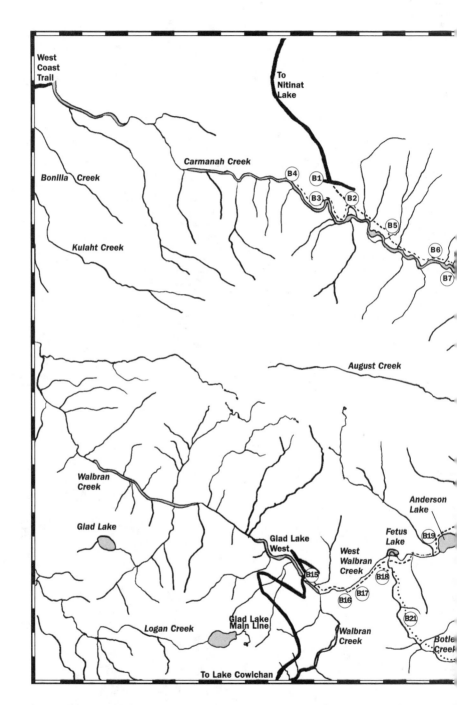

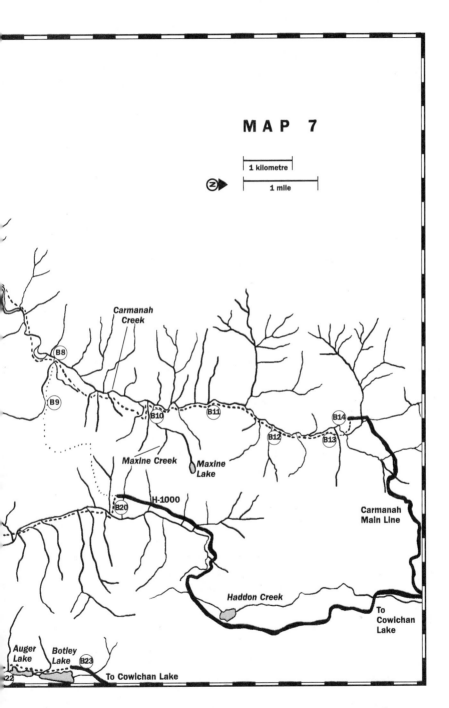

MAP 7

1 kilometre

1 mile

Carmanah
Creek

B8

B9

B10   B11

B14

B12   B13

Maxine Creek   Maxine
Lake

H-1000

B20

Carmanah
Main Line

Haddon Creek

To
Cowichan
Lake

Auger   Botley
Lake   Lake   B23

22   To Cowichan Lake

67

NOTES TO MAP 7

B1 *Carmanah–Walbran Provincial Park Headquarters. Parking lot and walk-in campsites off upper road. Outhouses and drinking water also available.*

B2 *Y-junction in the feature zone of the park. Boardwalk to many of the large Sitka spruce.*

B3 *Randy Stoltmann memorial grove.*

B4 *Trail ends. Access to the West Coast Trail and Carmanah Beach is no longer permitted.*

B5 *Three sisters, Sitka spruce grove. Beyond here the trail is not improved.*

B6 *Grunt's Grove campsite.*

B7 *Paradise Pool. Beautiful, deep swimming hole in the creek.*

B8 *Mystic's Hollow Camp. Near junction of August Creek and Carmanah Creek.*

B9 *Route to West Walbran ascends up August Creek and continues over ridge to drop down to West Walbran Creek. Route is not improved and is recommended for experienced hikers only.*

B10 *Sleepy Hollow Camp adjacent to Maxine Creek.*

B11 *Camp Patience. Steep side trail leads to waterfalls and pools of Carmanah Creek.*

B12 *Bear Paw Camp.*

B13 *Hummingbird Research Camp. Site of Western Canada Wilderness Committee research camp for old-growth forests and their species.*

B14 *Headwaters trailhead and junction with side logging road that connects with Carmanah Main Line. Limited parking available. Trail starts in new growth.*

B15 *Trailhead for West Walbran Trail. Begins in forest near logging bridge over Walbran Creek.*

B16 *Cable car crossing of West Walbran above Fletcher Falls.*

B17 *Giggling Spruce campsite.*

B18 *Trail junction. Central Walbran Trail bears to the left and continues up Botley Creek to Botley and Auger Lakes. Keep to the left for West Walbran Trail, Fetus Lake and Maxine's Tree.*

B19 *Anderson Lake campsite on gravel beach exposed at low water.*

B20 *H-1000 logging road, which connects to Haddon Creek Main Line. Trailhead for West Walbran Trail and route to Carmanah Creek.*

B21 *Route to Botley Lake is mostly unimproved trail and is recommended for experienced hikers only.*

B22 *Trail from Botley Creek ends and route continues to junction with West Walbran Trail.*

B23 *Trailhead to Botley and Auger Lakes. Access to logging road system, which connects with McLure Lake Main Line and Cowichan Lake.*

turns to the north at the top of the ridge that separates the two watersheds. Another 2 kilometres (about a mile) of bushwhacking will bring you to the spur logging road, H-1000, off Haddon Main Line. This is a trailhead for the start of the West Walbran Trail, which leads to Anderson Lake and farther along to the main stem of Walbran Creek. If you plan to hike this trail, bring a compass and topographic maps.

TRAILS IN THE WALBRAN VALLEY

There are three main trail systems in the Walbran Valley: the West Walbran Trail, the Central Walbran Trail and the Lower Walbran Trail. None of these trails is maintained by B.C. Parks. All trails were built by volunteers of the Carmanah Forestry Society in an attempt to promote the area before it was logged. Access to the main trail system is via McLure Lake Main Line to Glad Lake Main Line to Glad Lake West. Further details are given in Chapter 6. The trailhead to the West Walbran begins near the logging bridge over the main stem of Walbran Creek. Look for the start in the wooded area to the right of the bridge after you cross it. Parking is available off the logging road that continues to the left. An alternative approach to starting the trail is to cross the bridge and follow the logging road to the left and then to the right up a clear-cut slope as it switchbacks. A trail leads into the forest near the end of this spur road. The clear-cut area is not included within the park.

The West Walbran Trail ascends alongside Fletcher Falls. There are some side trails that give good views of the falls. A short distance past the falls, you reach a cable car crossing of the creek. At time of writing the car was in good shape. When you complete the crossing, the West Walbran Trail leads left in a northerly direction. If you turn to the right, you will hike for about twenty minutes to a huge red cedar.

The West Walbran Trail enters the park a few hundred metres after the cable car crossing. The trail is in rough shape in places and you can expect to encounter mud and many roots criss-crossing the trail. The first wilderness campsite is Giggling Spruce, in a small grove of large Sitka beside the creek. After a few kilometres of slogging you will cross the Central Walbran Creek, which is also called Botley Creek. There is no bridge crossing here, and you may have to wade the creek, depending on the amount of water flowing through. A short distance past this creek crossing you will reach a junction with the Central Walbran Trail

Beach, West Coast Trail. ADRIAN DORST

that leads to Auger Lake and Botley Lake. If you continue along the West Walbran Trail, you will catch glimpses of Fetus Lake, a shallow, marshy body of water to the west. One of the main attractions along the West Walbran Trail is Maxine's Tree, an enormous Sitka spruce named for the daughter of Syd Haskell, the founder of the Carmanah Forestry Society; he helped organize many of the volunteers who built the trails in this area.

The trail recrosses Walbran Creek to the west side shortly past Maxine's Tree and continues up to Anderson Lake. There is a good campsite on the gravel at the south end of the lake adjacent to a tributary's entrance into the lake. The trail tends to be a bit confusing in this area, and you may lose it. Basically, the path follows the west side of the lake, although you will be hiking up from the lake for most of the trip. At the head of Anderson Lake, the trail descends through a marshy area and meets a side stream. This stream may have to be waded in high water. The trail then crosses West Walbran Creek on a log to the east side. From this point, the route follows the stream through marsh, thicket and spruce forest. One final creek crossing awaits you near the trailhead; a log will take you across to the west side. Camp Perfection is found here nestled among the old growth. Access to the trailhead at H-1000 is described in Chapter 6. From this trailhead, if you are an experienced bushwhacker, you can continue to the Carmanah Valley as described above. The trailhead for the Central Walbran Trail is reached via McLure Lake Main Line and Walbran Main Line. Since the spur logging road off Walbran Main Line is rough, you may have to hike in the 2.5 kilometres (1.5 miles) to the trailhead. The trail crosses a small stream and reaches the shore of Botley Lake in a few minutes from trailhead. The path wends its way to Auger Lake. Midway down Auger Lake there is a grove of large western cedars. The trail dissipates to a rougher route after Auger Lake, and the experienced hiker will be able to reach its junction with the West Walbran Trail as outlined above.

The Lower Walbran Trail is reached after crossing the bridge from Glad Lake West over Walbran Creek. Turn left after the bridge. Continue down the logging road to its end. Drop down from the road to Walbran Creek, and you will pick the trail up near the creek. The trail meanders alongside the creek for some distance. It is rough and tricky going in parts.

It bears repeating that none of the trails in the Walbran Valley are maintained. You may encounter washouts and detours around fallen trees. It is easy to lose the trail in many sections. Thus, hiking in the Walbran is not recommended for novices.

CHAPTER SIX

Permits and Access

WEST COAST TRAIL AND NITINAT TRIANGLE

TRAIL PERMITS ARE REQUIRED FOR ALL overnight stays on the West Coast Trail between April 15 and October 1. Permit reservations may be made by phoning Discover BC reservation service at the following numbers:

1-800-663-6000 within Canada and the United States
250-387-1642 outside Canada and the United States
663-6000 in Greater Vancouver

Reservations may be made seven days a week, starting March 1, between 6:00 A.M. and 6:00 P.M. Pacific time. There is a non-refundable $25 fee per hiker for making reservations, which is payable with credit card (Visa and MasterCard only). Before you phone for a reservation you should know the date you want to begin your hike (with two alternative dates in case your chosen date is full), the trailhead where you intend to start (Pachena, Gordon River or Nitinat Lake), the mailing address of the group leader and the number of hikers in your group.

< Aerial view, West Coast Trail. ADRIAN DORST

The more popular dates for hiking, in July and August, fill up quite rapidly, so you should book as far in advance as possible. The maximum group size is fixed at ten persons. Only one commercial or organized group is permitted to start the trail every other day from either end of the trail.

You will receive a reservation confirmation number and a preparation guide when you register. Permits must be picked up at the Information Centre adjacent to your chosen trailhead before 1:00 P.M. on the date of your hike. You may collect your permit one day in advance if you wish to get an early start on the first day of your hike. If you fail to claim your permit before then, your reservation is automatically cancelled and your spot will be filled by someone on the waiting list.

The PRNP has a quota system in place. Only sixty hikers—twenty-six from Gordon River, twenty-six from Pachena Bay and eight from Nitinat—will be allowed to begin the trail on each day that the trail is officially open. Six spots each at the Gordon River and Pachena trailheads are available each day for those who arrive without a permit. Hikers who arrive at one of the trailheads without a reservation, however, may have to wait several days for an opening, particularly during the peak months of July and August. Waiting lists for those without permits operate on a first-come, first-served system. When you arrive at trailhead, you should present yourself at the Information Centre in order to be placed on the waiting list. Spaces are then allocated by the staff at the information centres at 1:00 P.M. each day. All hikers must register and receive a one-hour orientation session at the trailhead before they are issued a trail use permit.

At this time the fee for obtaining a trail use permit is $70 per person. This fee is in addition to the reservation fee and is payable at the time the permit is issued. You may pay by Visa, MasterCard, cash or traveller's cheques in the exact amount only. The fee is charged to help defray some of the costs of maintaining the trail and for some rescue services. Day hikers are not assessed a permit fee. Hikers who attempt the trail without a valid permit may be forced to leave the trail and may face court charges and fines.

Canoeists who wish to use the Nitinat Triangle are also required to obtain backcountry use permits before beginning their trip. At the present time there are no quotas in place for canoeing the Nitinat

Triangle. Permits are available at the Information Centre at the Ditidaht village at the eastern end of Nitinat Lake or at any of the other information centres. For up-to-date information about waiting lists and permit requirements for the West Coast Trail or Nitinat Triangle, you may phone the following numbers:

PRNP Headquarters 250-726-7721
Pachena Bay Information Centre 250-728-3234
Gordon River Information Centre 250-647-5434
Nitinat Lake Information Centre 250-745-8124

Transportation to and from the trailheads can be a problem to arrange. Most groups leave a car at either end of the trail. If you do this, allow a full day for travel. Alternatively, if you park your vehicle at trailhead, you may use one of the shuttle services that are described below to return to your vehicle.

The north end of the trail has better transportation facilities. The MV *Lady Rose* and the MV *Frances Barkley* operate as ferries between Bamfield and Port Alberni. At this writing the vessels operate on a year-round schedule between Bamfield and Port Alberni, leaving Port Alberni every Tuesday, Thursday and Saturday at 8:00 A.M. and reaching the Bamfield dock at 12:30 P.M. They leave Bamfield at 1:30 P.M. and arrive at Port Alberni at 5:30 P.M. There are additional summer sailings on Fridays and Sundays from July 1 through Labour Day (the first Monday in September). The Friday timetable is the same as the schedule given above for Tuesdays, Thursdays and Saturdays. On Sunday the boat departs at 8:00 A.M. and arrives at Bamfield at 1:30 P.M. The return voyage departs Bamfield at 3:00 P.M. and arrives at Port Alberni at 6:00 P.M. For further information and for reservations, which are highly recommended during the summer, call the following toll-free number during office hours from April through September: 1-800-663-7192. The local phone number in Port Alberni for Alberni Marine Transportation, which operates the *Lady Rose* and *Frances Barkley*, is 250-723-8313. If you do take one of these vessels, note that you will still have an hour's hike to get to the trailhead.

There is also a bus run by Western Bus Lines from late June until late September that links Bamfield and Port Alberni. It only runs on Mondays and Fridays, however, leaving Port Alberni at 12:45 P.M. and

75

arriving at Pachena Bay trailhead at 2:30 P.M. and at Bamfield fifteen minutes later. The return trip is on the same days at 3:00 P.M. from Bamfield (at the Bamfield Motel) and 3:15 P.M. at Pachena, with an arrival time in Port Alberni of 5:00 P.M. The phone number for up-to-date information and pickup locations in Port Alberni is 250-723-3341.

There are now two private bus shuttle services that can take you to either the Pachena trailhead or the Gordon River trailhead. The West Coast Trail Express can transport up to fifteen hikers and gear between Victoria, Nanaimo and the trailheads. It operates daily from early May to early October. For information, schedule and reservations, phone 250-477-8700. The Pacheenaht First Nation bus service uses air-conditioned vans to provide transportation between Port Renfrew, Nitinat and Bamfield. The phone numbers for reservation and departure times are 250-647-5521 or 250-647-5556.

Finally, there is the Juan de Fuca Express, a water taxi that cruises between Port Renfrew and Bamfield. It is run by Brian Gisborne, who is knowledgeable about the history of the West Coast Trail. If the weather and seas cooperate, you will be able to see many of the landmarks of the trail before or after your hike. For bookings and information, you can contact the Juan de Fuca Express at 1-888-755-6578 (toll-free in B.C. only) or 250-755-6578, or by e-mail at juanfuca@island.net.

If you have your own transportation, you will need to use logging roads to reach the Pachena Bay and Nitinat Lake trailheads. All of the main logging roads are open to the public twenty-four hours a day, but loaded logging trucks have the right-of-way. Expect to encounter logging trucks if you travel on weekdays between 6:00 A.M. and 6:00 P.M. You should drive with your headlights on at all times on logging roads. Remember also that logging roads are not well-maintained highways. You should expect to encounter blind corners, potholes and other hazards on your journey. No overnight camping is permitted on company-administered forest land except at designated camping sites.

Access to Port Renfrew is from Victoria via Highway 14 through Sooke and the Jordan River. Alternatively, you can reach Port Renfrew through Lake Cowichan and a logging road system that starts just after Honeymoon Bay. The logging road from Shawnigan Lake through the San Juan Valley to Port Renfrew is now closed because of a washed-out bridge about midway along the route. To reach the Information Centre and southern trailhead for the West Coast Trail, turn right before you reach the townsite of Port Renfrew. You will cross the bridge over the San Juan River and go through the Indian reserve. The Information Centre is located on the south bank of the Gordon River. There are few hotel and motel accommodations in Port Renfrew. There are a number of bed-and-breakfasts, however. If you plan to camp, the Pacheenaht First Nation has some camping sites and RV sites for rent on the reserve near the Information Centre. Should you wish to camp in town, there is a campsite run by Trailhead Resort close to the government dock. Trailhead Resort also operates a store that carries hiking and camping supplies in case you forgot something.

To begin the trail, you will need to be ferried across the Gordon River or across Port San Juan to Thrasher Cove. The PRNP staff advises that beginning in 1998 there will be no ferry access to Thrasher Cove. All hikers will begin the trail at the Gordon River. Pickup locations for the ferry, which is run by Butch Jack of the Pacheenaht First Nation, are near the Information Centre along the Gordon River and the government dock located just down from the Port Renfrew Hotel. For further information on this ferry service, phone 250-647-5517 or 250-647-5521.

To visit the Nitinat Lake Triangle or to reach the Nitinat Lake trailhead for access to the trail at its midpoint, you must travel along logging roads to the head of Nitinat Lake. From Victoria drive through Duncan and turn left off Highway 1 toward Lake Cowichan. Before you reach the town of Lake Cowichan turn right toward Youbou. The road becomes a gravel all-season road after you pass Youbou. At the head of Lake Cowichan turn left and then right to follow the signs for Caycuse and Nitinat Lake. You will eventually come to a major T-junction; looking right, you can see a bridge over the Nitinat River. The right-hand road goes to the west shore of Nitinat Lake and on to Bamfield or Port Alberni. The left-hand road leads to the east shore of Nitinat Lake and the Ditidaht village, where you will find the Information Centre in a trailer adjacent to the general store (the one with the gas pumps).

If you plan to hike the trail, you will pick up your permit and complete your orientation at the centre before heading off on boat transportation down Nitinat Lake to Whyac. At this writing the fee is $25 per person for the boat trip. You may wish to phone the Information Centre at the Ditidaht village for more information and pickup times.

77

The phone number for Carl Edgar, who operates the service, is 250-745-3509.

If you are planning to canoe the Nitinat Triangle, you should use the Knob Point picnic ground on the west shore of Nitinat Lake to launch your canoe. To reach this point, turn right at the T-junction, cross the bridge over the Nitinat River and turn left at the sign for the Nitinat Hatchery. After travelling 1.5 kilometres (about a mile) down this road you will see a sign for Knob Point, which is about 10 kilometres (6 miles) farther along the lakeshore. This site is preferable for launching your canoe to reach Hobiton Lake, since you do not have to canoe across Nitinat Lake. The logging road past Knob Point continues almost to Hobiton Creek but does not provide easy access to either Nitinat Lake or Hobiton Lake. Remember that Nitinat Lake has dangerous midday winds.

During the summer, the PRNP maintains a dock at the mouth of Nitinat Lake and requests that this dock be kept clear. If you have a large boat, it may either be anchored or pulled above the high-water mark—remember that Nitinat Lake is tidal. There is safe anchorage at Brown Bay.

Another route to the head of Nitinat Lake is via Port Alberni through Franklin Camp. A junction at the camp leads to either Nitinat Lake or to the west, Bamfield. If you are travelling to Bamfield from Victoria, use the Lake Cowichan route as described above. At the T-junction turn right over the Nitinat River Bridge, continue to Franklin Camp and follow the signs to Bamfield. Logging travel may be slow; you should allow about five hours to reach Bamfield from Victoria and about three hours to reach it from Port Alberni.

Access to the Pachena Bay trailhead starts about 5 kilometres (3 miles) before Bamfield along a short branch road to the left off the main road. There is a sign for the West Coast Trail at this location. If you arrive at a bridge over the Pachena River, you have missed this turn. Parking is available in the lot at the end of this side road. Do not leave valuables in your vehicle; thieves have been known to operate in this area. Bamfield has a few grocery stores, restaurants and motels. Fuel is also available at a few locations. Camping is available either near the trailhead on the beach or at the commercial campground on Pachena Bay on the Huu-Ay-Aht reserve.

JUAN DE FUCA MARINE TRAIL

Generally, access to the trailheads on this trail is easier. All trailheads are accessed off Highway 14 and are well marked by signs. If you are hiking in a group, allow some time to arrange cars at your planned destination. You will reach the first trailhead at China Beach a few kilometres after you pass through Jordan River. Use the first parking lot on the right as you exit the highway. You will reach the next trailhead, at Sombrio Beach, after you cross the bridge over Loss Creek. There is an old logging road that takes you downhill to a parking lot. The trailhead at Parkinson Creek is a few kilometres to the west of the Sombrio Beach trailhead. A logging road of approximately 4 kilometres (2.5 miles) takes you to a parking lot. You will intersect a number of logging roads on the route to this lot. As a general rule keep to the right at these intersections. To reach the Botanical Beach trailhead, travel through Port Renfrew. Turn left before you arrive at the Port Renfrew Hotel and the government dock. You will drive along a gravel road for approximately 3.5 kilometres (2 miles) before you reach the large parking lot for Botanical Beach and Botany Bay. All trailheads have large covered bulletin boards that list valuable information such as tides and bear and cougar sightings.

Public transportation to the trailheads on the Juan de Fuca Trail is available from Victoria on the West Coast Trail Express. A daily shuttle bus stops off at French Beach, China Beach and Port Renfrew. Further information and reservations are available by phoning 250-477-8700. The Pacheenaht First Nation offers a scheduled bus service for Sooke, Jordan River and the Juan de Fuca Trail. This service operates out of Port Renfrew and services all four trailheads on the Juan de Fuca Trail. For reservations and times, phone 250-647-5521 or 250-647-5556. Public bus transportation is available through B.C. Transit from Victoria to Sooke. Thus, you can link up with the Pacheenaht service from Sooke to your trailhead.

Finally, the Juan de Fuca Express marine taxi services this trail as well as the West Coast Trail. For bookings and information, phone 1-888-755-6578 (toll-free in B.C.) or 1-250-755-6578.

At time of this writing hiking permits are not required for the Juan de Fuca Trail. There is an overnight camping fee, however, for each night you plan to camp on the trail. The fee is $6 per night per party of

79

Loss Creek Suspension Bridge, Juan de Fuca Trail. BO MARTIN

four. The permit is obtained as a self-registration system from any of the trailheads. A fine of $50 may be assessed if you camp without such a permit.

CARMANAH–WALBRAN PROVINCIAL PARK

At the present time there are no public transportation services to this park. You will need a vehicle with good tires and good traction to reach any of the hiking trails in this area. To reach the lower Carmanah Valley, where you will find a campground as well as the majority of the large trees in the feature zone, follow the directions given above for Nitinat Lake. Drive past the Ditidaht village at Nitinat Lake and continue along South Main Line until you reach the Caycuse River Bridge. You may encounter a safety checkpoint here. You should stop for information and to obtain the operator's instructions. The operator is in radio contact with logging trucks in the vicinity and will advise the drivers of your presence. Turn right after crossing the bridge and go along Rosander Main Line logging road for about 30 kilometres (19 miles). The road will climb steadily as you traverse Nitinat Lake before heading down and turning left for the Carmanah Valley.

To reach the upper Carmanah Valley, turn left after you cross the

Caycuse River Bridge onto West Haddon Main Line. After you travel about 10 kilometres (6 miles), this road splits at a forked junction, where you will take a right onto Carmanah Main Line. From here it is approximately 5 kilometres (3 miles) to the parking lot for the Headwaters trailhead. As a general rule, keep to the left along Carmanah Main Line at various intersections.

The road will dip down to cross Carmanah Creek. Take the first left after this bridge and travel about 600 metres (650 yards) to the end of the road. The trail to the upper Carmanah is located off the road to the left and travels through scrub and brush before you reach a bridge over Carmanah Creek.

To reach the main trail system of the Walbran, follow the south side of Cowichan Lake past Honeymoon Bay. Just past Caycuse Camp turn left along Caycuse Main Line until you reach a junction with McClure Lake Main Line and continue along this road until you reach McClure Lake. At the junction at the end of the lake take the left fork onto Glad Lake Main Line and continue for several kilometres until you reach Glad Lake West. Turn right and cross a bridge over the eastern branch of Walbran Creek. Continue up the hill and then descend to cross the main stem of the Walbran. The trail along the main stem of the Walbran and the West Walbran Trail start near the bridge.

To reach the Central Walbran trailhead near Botley Lake follow the instructions above until you reach the Y-junction at the end of McClure Lake. Take the left fork onto Walbran Main Line and follow it for 2 kilometres (a little over a mile) to another Y-junction. The left fork leads down to Botley Lake. Keep to the left at any intersection. At this writing the road was washed out, so exercise caution when travelling along it.

To reach the West Walbran trailhead, follow the above instructions for Walbran Main Line, but keep to the right at the second Y-junction (the left takes you down to Botley Lake). Turn left onto Haddon Main Line and continue for 5 kilometres (3 miles) until you cross a narrow bridge. Continue straight ahead to a Y-junction, where you will take the right fork marked H-1000. You will find the trailhead at the end of the road.

Hole in the Wall, West Coast Trail. BO MARTIN

CHAPTER SEVEN

Equipment
and Provisions

FOR BACKPACKERS THERE IS PERHAPS NO topic more controversial than what type of equipment to use for a hike. Hikers have been known to hold discourse for hours on the relative merits of synthetic versus natural fill or internal versus external frame packs. This chapter is not about such choices but about the selection of adequate gear and food to enable you to be self-sufficient on your hike. Whether you plan to hike one of the longer coast trails, such as the West Coast Trail, or to take a day trip along the Carmanah, you should plan your trip and be prepared for any emergency or weather condition that is likely to arise on your trek. Lack of proper equipment can turn a pleasurable hike into an ordeal. Weather along the west coast can range from cold winds and torrential rains to hot, bone-dry and sun-baked days when small streams have all disappeared. Most of the really bad weather occurs during the winter, but summer hikers should still expect rain and biting insects. Your gear must also be suited to the terrain that you are likely to encounter along the way. Wet and slippery logs, rocks and boardwalks; muddy paths; fogged glasses; and vertical ladders that seem to go on forever are all part of the coastal hiking experience. Once again, if you are prepared for these encounters, they will be challenges rather than potential sources of injury or illness.

The backpacker's challenge is to keep down the weight without sacrificing any of the items and foodstuffs that are essential for an enjoyable trip. As a general rule, you should not carry more than one-third of your body weight. This rule depends a lot on your age and physical shape. Experience in hiking is also a valuable asset that weighs nothing but usually sees one through the hard goings. Most of the hikes described in this book (with the exception of those in the central Carmanah Valley) are not for the novice hiker.

What you will need to carry for an extended backpacking trip can be broken down into five categories: general equipment (the hardware necessary to protect you from the elements), clothing, cooking and eating utensils, food and optional gear. I have not included any brand names, since personal tastes differ so widely. I would, however, urge you to purchase or rent only high-quality gear that can withstand the rigours of the trail. The following lists are intended as a guide.

GENERAL EQUIPMENT
- ☐ pack (waterproof or with waterproof pack cover)
- ☐ waterproof stuff sacks or heavy-duty garbage bags
- ☐ tent (with waterproof fly)
- ☐ sleeping bag (synthetic fill preferable to down)
- ☐ ground sheet (optional—depends on make of tent)
- ☐ fire-starting kit (explained in text)
- ☐ knife
- ☐ repair kit (for clothes, tent and pack)
- ☐ 15 metres (50 feet) of 7-millimetre rope
- ☐ tide tables
- ☐ flashlight (with spare batteries)
- ☐ candles (for light and for starting a fire)
- ☐ compass (if you plan to leave the trail)
- ☐ watch
- ☐ maps
- ☐ first-aid kit (essential)
- ☐ insect repellent
- ☐ sunscreen
- ☐ toiletries
- ☐ day pack (optional)

☐ cash (for ferry crossings—check with the PRNP for expected amounts)
☐ walking stick or hiking poles (optional)

Sharing some or these items can lighten individual loads. If you are hiking in a large group, however, be sure that there is adequate equipment for the entire group.

There are many types of backpacks on the market. You should compare them and consult someone experienced in backpacking before purchasing one. Most packs are not waterproof, so you should either purchase a cover for your pack or stow your food and clothing in stuff sacks or heavy-duty garbage bags before placing them in your pack.

Sleeping bags with synthetic fill are better than down-filled ones, since they absorb less moisture and dry more quickly. Your sleeping bag should have a waterproof stuff sack and be effective to approximately 0°C (32°F).

The fire-starting kit consists of waterproof matches and/or butane lighters plus fire-starter material. Some form of fire starter (waxed wood sticks work really well, or use the stub end of a candle) is essential, since much of the wood along the trail may be wet. Place a candle stub or a small tea candle under a teepee of kindling and let the candle burn until the wood catches.

You can assemble a small repair kit consisting of needles and thread for repairing cloth. For repairing your pack, take along a couple of metres of flexible wire and lightweight pliers (a multi-purpose tool usually functions equally well). Your repair kit should also contain some heavy string and duct tape. Plastic bags are also useful for storing items in your pack and keeping matches and toilet paper dry. A flashlight with spare batteries comes in handy for those evenings when you are trying to pitch your tent in the dark. Candles with a good candle lantern are good for that warm glow in the tent for reading.

If you are hiking the West Coast Trail, the waterproof map produced by the B.C. Ministry of the Environment, Lands and Parks is excellent. You may buy a copy of this map at the information centres, and one is included in your preparation kit if you have reserved a date for your trail start. Another plastic-coated map for the West Coast Trail is published by International Travel Maps of Vancouver and is available from many outdoor stores in the Vancouver area and on Vancouver Island. This map also includes the Nitinat Triangle and the Carmanah–Walbran

Provincial Park. If you are hiking the Juan de Fuca Trail, TRIM (Terrain Resource Information Management Program) maps provide a wealth of detail. These maps are available from Ministry of the Environment via the Internet at www.env.gov.bc.ca/srmb/trim.htm. B.C. Parks also produces a free map of the trail, but the scale is not very detailed. A copy may be obtained by contacting B.C. Parks at 250-391-2300.

Your first-aid kit should be well stocked for a long hike. There are several commercially prepared kits, or you can make up your own. First-aid knowledge and training is important to obtain before your trip.

A small container of insect repellent is essential during the summer. Biting insects are usually not plentiful on the beach; when you walk away from the sea breezes, however, you will discover that there are indeed mosquitoes and black flies along the coast. The repellent should contain DEET to be effective. If you want to "go organic," try garlic instead of the chemicals. I don't vouch for its effectiveness, but you may find that if you ingest enough, you won't be bothered by pests of either the six-legged or the two-legged variety. Sunscreen with PABA or zinc oxide as the blocking agent should be carried if you are either an optimist or a sun lover or both.

A light day pack or fanny pack is useful if you plan to establish a base camp and take day trips from it.

A walking stick or collapsible hiking poles are useful for most of the terrain encountered along coastal trails. These items are invaluable along slippery boardwalks and help maintain balance during stream crossings. Many hikers use a pair of poles, particularly those hikers who suffer from knee ailments.

CLOTHING
- ☐ boots (waterproofed in advance)
- ☐ 3 pairs of socks
- ☐ gaiters
- ☐ trousers (preferably pile or wool)
- ☐ hiking shorts
- ☐ waterproof outerwear
- ☐ waterproof hat (with wide brim for both sun and rain)
- ☐ underwear
- ☐ shirts

☐ sweater or fleece jacket
☐ gloves (optional for summer months)
☐ rubber sandals (for stream crossings)
☐ sunglasses

Clothing should be chosen for utility, warmth and weight. Some hikers prefer to put on a set of clean clothes every morning, whereas others will wear the same clothes every day and thus leave room in their pack for optional items such as a book or a camera.

Footwear is perhaps the most critical item on this list. The PRNP reports that wearing inadequate footwear such as runners or light hiking boots causes most of the injuries along the West Coast Trail. Knee injuries are most frequent, closely followed by ankle injuries.

Boots should provide good ankle and arch support. Vibram soles or the equivalent are probably the best for the many types of terrain that you will encounter along the trail. Your boots should be well broken in and waterproofed before you start. All outdoor stores stock a number of brands of waterproofing agents to match the composition of your boot. Split leather (suede) boots are not recommended, since they are difficult to keep waterproofed. You should also carry along a pair of high-quality rubber sandals for stream crossings and use around the campsite. These should be well constructed with strong Velcro straps and should provide good traction on slippery rocks.

Proper socks can help prevent blisters. Wearing thin socks as inner liners wicks away perspiration and helps cut down on chafing. Outer socks are heavier and should be padded in the heel and toe area for extra comfort. You can expect to have wet feet along the trail unless you wear a good pair of gaiters. These should be high quality and have a strap for securing the gaiter under the insole of your boot. Waterproof material for the lower portions combined with a breathable water-resistant material for the upper part of the gaiter works best.

Wearing jeans while hiking is strongly discouraged. When wet, jeans become heavy and lose their ability to insulate. Choose a quick-drying pair of pants or simply wear shorts under waterproof pants.

Rain gear is essential. Take along a loose-fitting jacket and a pair of trousers that have long enough side zips to allow you to put them on without first removing your boots. The choice of material for such a rain suit is one of the more controversial issues around gear selection for any backpacker. You should consult a number of knowledgeable people and read articles that compare products (often found in magazines such as *Backpacker*) before purchasing your rain gear. The trade-off is between waterproofness, which keeps you dry but clammy, and breathability, which eliminates internal moisture but may allow leaking during the pelting torrents of rain that frequently occur on the coast.

A wide-brimmed hat is a good addition to your backpacking wardrobe; it will keep the sun off your face and the rain out of your eyes. Some hikers take along a toque for chilly nights.

The principle of layering is very effective for the variable climate you will encounter along your trip. Wearing several layers of warm lighter clothing instead of a single layer of heavy clothing allows you to take off or add layers as the weather changes.

Fleece jackets are warm, shed water and dry rapidly. They are excellent choices in either a zip-up or pullover model. Trousers and socks made out of fleece material are also good choices for warm clothing. Once again, you must choose between being warm but carrying the extra weight of several articles of clothing and travelling light but possibly being cold.

COOKING AND EATING UTENSILS
- ☐ stove
- ☐ fuel
- ☐ pots
- ☐ cup
- ☐ plate or bowl
- ☐ fork and spoon
- ☐ knife (a general-purpose pocketknife is good for both food and trail use)
- ☐ plastic garbage bags
- ☐ pot scrubber and biodegradable soap
- ☐ water bottle
- ☐ water filter (optional)

Although campfires are permitted on the beaches of the coastal hikes, you cannot always rely on a fire for cooking. A lightweight stove that burns white gas (naphtha petroleum) and has a pump system is thus an essential item on your equipment list. Be sure to bring enough fuel. Most hikers warm up some hot water in the morning for tea or porridge. And remember that dinners take longer to cook than other meals. Estimate your fuel consumption for the number of meals you will be cooking and then add extra fuel to be sure you won't run out.

The larger the group size, the larger the number and size of pots you should take along. For small groups (four or less), you can get by with two pots—a 4-litre pot and a 2-litre pot are usually adequate for most purposes. If you are a gourmet cook, you will probably want to check out the backpacking utensils that are available at most outdoor stores. Everything from backcountry ovens for baking bread to wilderness espresso makers is on the market. Remember that each one of these items means additional weight to your burgeoning pack.

Water filters are now widely used to deal with increasing problems with the quality of water from streams. The presence of *Giardia lamblia*, a microorganism that may cause stomach cramps and diarrhea, is suspected in some of the streams along the coast. Other streams are beginning to show the presence of *Escherichia coli*, which can also cause health ailments. Thus you should boil your water, treat it with chemicals or filter it. Some bodies of water, such as the Nitinat, Cheewhat, Klanawa and Walbran, are brackish and unsuitable for drinking. Boiling such water does not purify it but rather makes it more saline.

FOOD

Planning and some ingenuity are the critical ingredients in producing satisfying and economical meals on the trail. Lightweight freeze-dried food is available, but it tends to be expensive. A visit to the pasta or rice sections of the supermarket should give you some indication of what is available for dinner along the trail. You should try to find items that are light in weight and take little cooking time. In order to replenish your calories lost to exercise, you should stock up on carbohydrates and high-energy foods. In addition to meals, you will want to carry trail foods such as energy bars and trail mix.

In planning your group meals, remember to pack sauces, spices and seasonings. Most hikers build up enormous appetites, so plan on extra food consumption. Always carry an extra day's worth of meals in case you run behind your intended schedule as a result of unforeseen difficulties.

OPTIONAL GEAR

What you take besides necessities depends on your experience, strength, pack size and interests. You may wish to take along a compact camera to visually record your journey. A small pair of binoculars is also useful for observing wildlife such as sea lions and whales that are offshore. There is usually room in your pack for a good book or deck of cards if you are so inclined.

Inveterate anglers will want to bring along fishing rods; a compact spin casting rig is most suitable. You will need a licence for both tidal and freshwater fishing for many of the areas covered by this guide. A Parks Canada fishing licence is required for fishing along the West Coast Trail.

CHAPTER EIGHT

Practical Advice

ERE IS MORE TO HIKING THAN proper gear and the right maps. Hiking the coastal trails in this book involves travelling through wilderness. A certain "wilderness ethic" is required for camping. Your aim should be to leave no trace of your passage through the pristine beauty. The adages "Pack it in—pack it out" and "Take nothing but photos—leave nothing but footprints" apply to the trails in this guide. For that reason you must practise no-trace camping. You should consider camping without a fire.

Hiking in the wilderness also involves a certain amount of common sense. Some of the trails in this guide are not heavily used during the summer, and all of the trails described here are seldom visited in the winter. Thus, you should always advise close friends or relatives of your itinerary and expected date for finishing a hike. The number of rescues on the West Coast Trail has increased dramatically over the last few years. Often injuries are caused by hikers hurrying along the trail. Although the West Coast Trail can be hiked in a few days, there is no need for such speed. The enjoyment of a wilderness setting is a part of the experience. None of the hikes described in this book are meant to be endurance tests or competitive races. Take the time to observe nature and enjoy the experience.

Leaders of the group have a special duty to ensure that the group stick together. The slowest members are usually the least experienced, and they are the ones most likely to encounter injuries. Everyone should be properly equipped and prepared to deal with emergency situations.

Probably the greatest danger to poorly equipped or inexperienced hikers is hypothermia, a term that means "low body temperature." It is especially likely to occur when dampness is combined with cold, a situation for which the west coast of Vancouver Island is well known, even in midsummer. You can get so cold that your body's normal means of regulating temperature, such as blood vessel contraction, shivering and fast respiration, all fail. If you reach this point, your presence of mind also fails and you are prone to making bad decisions instead of taking the drastic action necessary to restore body heat. An early symptom of hypothermia is prolonged shivering. The later, more serious symptoms are connected with the loss of self-control: poor muscle coordination, weakness, slurred speech and impaired judgment. From this juncture, it is downhill to coma and death unless appropriate action is taken immediately.

The best treatment for hypothermia is prevention: being equipped with adequate rain gear and warm clothing. If hypothermia does occur to someone in your party, rescuers must remember that a person suffering from hypothermia has lost the ability to generate body heat and must be supplied with heat from an external source. This source could include the warmth from a campfire, gently inhaled steam, warm (but not scalding hot) liquids or another person's body heat. Merely wrapping a person in warm clothing or a sleeping bag may be useless—an innocent mistake that has cost lives.

Coastal hiking involves the diurnal cycle of tides. Throughout this guide reference is made to hiking along the beach if the tide is low enough. Tide tables are critical for hiking the coast. At this writing, staff at the information centres for the West Coast Trail will provide you with the tide tables for the dates of your hike. Remember that times are given in standard time, so you must add an hour for daylight saving time.

If predicting tides is critical (for example, when you are paddling through Nitinat Narrows or hiking a stretch of coast where you could be trapped by an incoming tide), you must interpolate from reference ports to secondary ports. Details are found in *Canadian Tide and Current Tables*, Volume 6, available from most marine retail outlets. This publication also gives current tables for Nitinat Bar. Remember that tide and current tables are only predictions, and various circumstances can cause them to be inaccurate. Do not stake your life on their absolute accuracy.

There are several locations where you will have to cross a stream on foot. If the stream is fast flowing, a stave is essential for balance. High-quality sandals are also useful for the slippery rocks you will likely encounter in stream crossing. If there is a possibility of being swept out to sea, use ropes and send one hiker across at a time. If everyone moves into the water at once, there is a danger that if one person falls, the entire group may be swept out to sea.

The trails in this guide are also home to two large mammals—cougar and black bear. Of the two, the black bear is the more common critter and the one you are more likely to meet. You can avoid potentially dangerous situations if you follow a number of precautions.

- Always make noise in an area frequented by bear. Wear bear bells, clap or talk loudly.
- Do not approach or feed bears or any other wild creature. Do not provoke them either.
- Store all of your food in caches high in a tree. Do not store any food or toiletries in your tent. Bears tend to be nocturnal creatures and have been known to invade tents in search of food that is inside.
- If you encounter a black bear on the trail, back away slowly. Do not turn your back on the animal. Do not run away or wave your arms at it. If a black bear attacks you, do not play dead. You should fight back and use whatever weapon is available to fend off its attack. Bear spray and bear bangers are two devices that may prove to be useful in avoiding an attack.
- Avoid cubs at all times.

The same warnings apply to cougar encounters, although these are rarer and the cougar is a less predictable animal than the black bear. Most of the time, a black bear or cougar will run away from you.

Dogs and bicycles are not allowed on the West Coast Trail.

Sitka spruce along the Juan de Fuca Trail. ADRIAN DORST

CHAPTER NINE

Flora and Fauna

FOUR MAIN SPECIES OF LARGE CONIFERS are commonly found along the hikes described in this book: Douglas-fir, western hemlock, western red cedar and Sitka spruce. These trees thrive on the west coast of Vancouver Island, grow to enormous size and are long-lived; some are as much as a thousand years old. Douglas-fir, *Pseudotsuga menziesi*, is generally found in younger, more open forests than the other species. This species is distinguished by cones with three-pronged bracts and has thick, ridged bark. Sitka spruce, *Picea sitchensis*, is found along the coast and up some of the valleys, such as the Carmanah and Walbran Valleys. This species has scaly bark and very sharp needles. If you grab onto a branch and the needles dig into the skin of your palm, chances are good that you have hold of a Sitka spruce. The boughs of this tree were used in ceremonial dances by the Nuu-chah-nulth people in this area to ward off evil spirits. Spruce is tolerant of salt water and is thus found close to the shoreline.

Away from the exposed coast, western hemlock, *Tsuga heterophylla*, and western red cedar, *Thuja plicata*, are the dominant species. Hemlock is distinguished by a drooping crown with graceful boughs, flat small needles and relatively smooth bark. This species tolerates shade and will grow beneath other species of trees. Cedar has ropy reddish-brown bark. It is perhaps the most important tree in the coastal Native culture and is the official tree of British Columbia. First Nations people used the wood for longhouses and totem poles. Seedlings are tolerant of shade and are found in the understorey of mature forests. Cedar burns well even when wet and is quite aromatic. You will find the occasional pine tree, *Pinus contorta*, along the coast in areas that lack groundwater. In young forests, such as the one west of Sombrio, you will find deciduous species of trees, especially red alder and maple.

The understorey of the rain forest is too diverse to describe here. It is thickest in the open areas and sparser in the dark, mature forest. Salal is the most common west coast shrub; it ranges from low ground cover to impenetrable jungle, sometimes growing to a height of 2.5 metres (8 feet). Salmonberry is thick in many areas, and its berries (red when ripe; salmon/orange when not) will provide a quick snack along many of the paths. Other edible berries in this area include huckleberry, thimbleberry and wild blackberry. Numerous ferns are found in shaded, damp forest and moist banks of streams.

In the bogs you will find a diversity of plant species quite different from the ones found in the rain forest. Of particular interest are the insectivorous plants, the sundews. Trees are usually stunted because of the nutrient-poor environment. Shore pine and yellow cedar are commonly found in these areas. Sphagnum mosses and other species of moss also abound in this wet zone.

Along the coast, a great variety of seaweed is visible in the ocean at low tide. One remarkable species is the sea palm, *Postelsia*, which clings to the rocks at the most turbulent part of the low-tide zone. It is an impressive sight to watch the sea palm bend under the impact of huge breakers and then spring back intact after the wave has passed. There are too many plants and animals within the intertidal zone to discuss here. Take along a good guidebook if you are interested in the fascinating life of a tide pool. Several such books are listed in the bibliography.

Not many large animals are spotted along the coast trails, since the forest is usually so thick. Black-tailed deer, black bear and cougar are sometimes sighted, however. Both California and Steller's sea lions are found offshore along the coast. Steller's sea lions are more commonly spotted—they are generally larger and blonder than the California sea lion and growl rather than bark. Seal lions are best spotted near the Pachena lighthouse and the Carmanah lighthouse offshore on rocky islets.

Harbour seals and river otters are commonly observed in Nitinat Lake.

Small animals such as squirrels, raccoons and minks are more abundant than the larger ones. Several types of mice frequent camping spots. You may discover signs of their presence if you leave food in your pack rather than in a food cache up a tree.

Bird life is rich; eagles are common, as are aquatic and marine species of birds such as loons, mergansers and gulls. The marbled murrelet has become a symbol of the Carmanah Valley since a nest was first discovered there. It is a small seabird that fishes by day in the ocean and returns to nest in the high branches of tall trees in the old-growth forest. With the increasing disappearance of its nesting habitat, the marbled murrelet has become rare. If you are an avid bird watcher, Parks Canada produces a handy checklist of the more than 250 species of birds that may be spotted in Pacific Rim National Park.

There are a number of salmon spawning runs in the streams along the coast. Sockeye, chum and coho salmon spawn in Hobiton Lake. The fish in this creek-lake system spawn in gravel along the perimeter of Hobiton Lake rather than in the streambed. If you are in this area in the fall, take care when choosing your campsite. The sockeye in the Cheewhat system are unusual because the spawners return throughout the year rather than at one time. This was an important factor for the First Nations who settled the area. The chum salmon fishery of the Doobah was once the richest along the coast. Through a combination of overfishing and improper logging practices, the salmon were eliminated from this creek. The same pattern has been repeated for many of the streams along the coast; particularly hard hit have been the chinook and coho species of salmon.

The taking or disturbing of wildlife is expressly prohibited in any of the parks described in this guide. This ban applies to all shellfish, including mussels and crab. All living creatures and plants as well as their fossilized remains are forbidden to be removed.

During the summer a phenomenon known as red tide may occur. Eating filter-feeding mollusks and shellfish during a red tide can result in a potentially fatal disease called paralytic shellfish poisoning (PSP). There may be a notice at the information centres at the West Coast or Juan de Fuca trailheads about shellfish closures in the area. Phone the Department of Fisheries and Oceans in Port Alberni (250-723-4524) for up-to-date information on red tide and closures.

CHAPTER TEN

First Nations

THERE ARE THREE SEPARATE FIRST NATIONS whose traditional homeland is the southwest coast of Vancouver Island. The Pacheenaht reside near Port Renfrew, the Ditidaht in the Nitinat Lake area and the Huu-Ay-Aht at Pachena Bay and Cape Beale. All three groups are part of the Nuu-chah-nulth language group. These people were mistakenly called Nootka for many years. The Nuu-chah-nulth are divided into three language groups: the northern and central groups speak dialects of one language, while the Ditidaht are linguistically more related to the Makah of the Olympic Peninsula. The Ditidaht and Pacheenaht First Nations speak a similar dialect, while the Huu-Ay-Aht are more closely related to the northern Nuu-chah-nulth groups.

The Nuu-chah-nulth were famed canoe builders. Various Native groups carved the large cedar trees that are found in the rain forest into seagoing canoes for pursuing whales and halibut. Of all the northwestern groups of Natives, only the Nuu-chah-nulth ventured far out to sea in pursuit of gray and humpback whales. The name Nuu-chah-nulth means "all along the mountains," which refers to the image of

< Cheewhat Beach, West Coast Trail. ADRIAN DORST

their homeland when they were returning to Vancouver Island after being far out at sea. Pacheenaht means "children of the sea foam," for these people used to travel far out to the Swiftsure Banks from Cullite Cove to catch halibut.

These three groups have reserve lands along the West Coast Trail and Nitinat Triangle, and the reserve lands near Port Renfrew, Clo-oose, Whyac, the Hobiton River, the Ditidaht village on Nitinat Lake and Pachena Bay are all inhabited. Other reserve lands are uninhabited. All reserve lands are clearly marked on the maps of the area. They are private lands, and no trespassing is permitted through these lands even if they are unoccupied. Although portions of the trail may pass through a reserve, you must remain on the trail. No camping or removal of wood is allowed unless you have the consent of members of the First Nation.

The West Coast Trail is patrolled by guardians of the Quu'as Group. Quu'as personnel come from the three First Nations and provide services such as ferry crossings at Nitinat Narrows and the Gordon River. They are also engaged in orientation for hikers, trail repair and maintenance, and protection of cultural resources. Cabins that house Quu'as guardians are located near Tsocowis Creek, Tsuquadra Creek and Camper Bay. Do not bother the staff unless you have an emergency or wish to report a serious problem with a trail.

In the future the PRNP will co-manage the West Coast Trail and Nitinat Lake Triangle with the First Nations.

CHAPTER ELEVEN

Conservation

V ANCOUVER ISLAND IS THE FIRST PLACE in British Columbia
where the myth of inexhaustible plenty has been completely
unmasked. The southern part of the island has seen logging
interests advanced to the exclusion of other uses of the land and, as a
result, the land base for recreation and preservation purposes has been
severely diminished.

In the 1950s, when Justice Sloan chaired two Royal Commissions of
Inquiry into the forest industry, his main conclusion was that Crown
forests should be managed to allow sustained yield. To implement this
program, the B.C. Forest Service, which lacked the finances and staff
to directly administer all of the Crown forest land, established many
areas as Tree Farm Licences (TFL), which were then leased to major logging companies. In this way, virtually all the forested Crown land on
Vancouver Island was committed to logging; very little attention was
paid to future recreational and preservationist needs. At the provincial
level, the existing parks system on Vancouver Island is essentially all
the public will have access to (with some few exceptions for company-
sponsored recreational sites) unless the government is prepared to
turn over areas committed to logging. And even when the province
does make a commitment to conserve wilderness values, as it has

attempted to do with the Protected Areas Strategy on Vancouver Island, the major logging companies look to the province for compensation for removal of timber from their TFLS and other forestry-based tenures.

The history of the conservation efforts to preserve the West Coast Trail and the Nitinat Triangle exemplifies a classic struggle over land use. When the Pacific Rim National Park was created in 1969, the boundaries of the trail were provisionally set as a kilometre-wide (0.6-mile-wide) strip except for enlargements at Cape Beale and Clo-oose. These boundaries are too narrow to protect the character of the West Coast Trail and at the time entirely omitted the Nitinat Lake area, an area of exceptional recreation potential and scientific interest. Other attractive areas, such as Black Lake and the Klanawa Valley, were also omitted. In 1970, the National Parks Branch requested that the province include the Nitinat Triangle in the proposed national park. The province, prodded by MacMillan Bloedel and B.C. Forest Products (now Timber West after several corporate transformations), which were the holders of the TFLS in the area, balked. This was the beginning of the local conflict between logging companies and conservationists. Over the years between 1970 and 1992, when the West Coast Trail and Nitinat Lake officially became part of Pacific Rim National Park, there have been much discussion and negotiation over compensation to the logging companies by way of land trades. The difficulty has always been finding suitable land bases on Vancouver Island to trade to the major companies for loss of cutting rights. Those trades have now been made and private land holdings around Clo-oose have also been relinquished to the Crown and are now part of the national park. In addition, Ditidaht land claims around the Nitinat Lake area have been resolved. So the boundaries of the park have been set and the land base fixed.

Nevertheless, the corridor allotted to the West Coast Trail is not wide enough to fully protect this ecosystem. The strip varies in width, with an average of just under a kilometre (0.6 mile). This width is not enought to prevent the encroachment of trails from logging roads near Bonilla Point and Sandstone Creek. In fact the sound of chain saws near Sandstone and Camper Creeks reverberates through the forest along the trail in those locations. It is difficult to have a wilderness experience with the sound of logging activities buzzing in one's ears.

And when the companies have done their work, one of the inevitable results of leaving a zone of clear-cut land behind a narrow strip of forest is to create a blowdown effect in the forest. The heavy sea winds rush into the vacuum created by the clear-cut and push over the trees standing in the way. Evidence of this blowdown effect is already seen between Camper Bay and Sandstone Creek. Further evidence can be seen on the Juan de Fuca Trail between Payzant Creek and Sombrio River. In contrast, the corridor allotted to the beach trail at Olympic National Park in Washington averages 5 kilometres (3 miles) in width.

After the struggle to have the West Coast Trail and the Nitinat Lake area set aside as parkland had been resolved, the focus on southern Vancouver Island shifted to the Carmanah and Walbran watersheds. In theory a watershed represents a complete ecosystem. Although there are certain components of such an ecosystem that may range outside the boundaries encompassed within the drainage, for the main part the plant species and smaller creatures form a cohesive system. Environmentalists as well as ecologists and scientists recognized the need to preserve some of the original, mature old-growth watersheds on the west coast of the Island. These forests have evolved over centuries, and many groups and individuals wanted them to be preserved before they were forever lost to the corporate interests of the logging companies that held the rights to the timber.

In the early 1990s public interest peaked and the lower Carmanah was set aside as a provincial park. The discovery of the first marbled murrelet nest in Canada in the Walbran Valley galvanized efforts by environmental groups to include the upper Carmanah and Walbran Valleys as parkland. In 1995 their efforts were rewarded through the creation of the Carmanah–Walbran Provincial Park, which contains two wholly protected watersheds within its confines: Logan and Cullite Creeks. And yet compared with the former old-growth paradise of the entire west coast of Vancouver Island, the amount of land base preserved is paltry.

Disputes such as those in the Walbran and Carmanah Valleys often come down to a question of the "best" economic use of land. Tourism and recreation needs on southwestern Vancouver Island have kept pace with the increasing demands of the logging companies for timber. The very fact that the PRNP has instituted a much needed quota system to limit the number of hikers on the West Coast Trail is evidence that the recreational demand in this area has far outstripped the availability of similar wilderness experiences.

Logging companies are quick to point out that decreasing the amount of timber that they are allowed to cut often translates into a reduction of jobs. But keeping the cut allowances high is only a short-term solution to the inevitable loss of logging jobs on southern Vancouver Island. Many experts predict that within the next two decades virtually all timber available for logging in this area will be exhausted.

In contrast, should the forests be available for use by scientists, recreational users and conservationists, then its value could be spread out over several generations in perpetuity. More than ten thousand people are drawn to the West Coast Trail and environs each year. These people contribute heavily to the economy of Port Renfrew, Port Alberni and Bamfield, with various spin-off effects on the rest of southern Vancouver Island. Thus, when one compares the long-term economic effects of tourism and recreational use of old-growth forests of southern Vancouver Island with logging, it is clear that over the long term, preservation of the forests is much more economically viable than clear-cutting them.

Moreover, we are only just beginning to grasp the significance of the disappearance of old growth and the dwindling numbers of salmon. Although the whole issue of the reduction of salmon species is complicated by other demands on the fish, including international disputes that may lead to overfishing, one of the recognized reasons for their decline is habitat destruction. The provincial government has attempted to address this problem by making changes to forest practices through the Forest Practices Code and by protecting fish habitat through the Fish Protection Act. And yet the monitoring of active logging on Vancouver Island suggests some early conclusions that logging companies are ignoring some of the more stringent restrictions placed on them for environmental reasons. At present the companies are complaining about the increased cost that would result if they were forced to totally comply with the code.

In addition, the demand for wilderness experience on southern Vancouver Island has increased even as the hectares of remaining old-growth forest have decreased. An increase in tourism does create problems in wilderness use, such as the quota system for the West Coast

Trail. To reduce this pressure, areas in addition to the West Coast Trail have been set aside. The creation of the Juan de Fuca Trail and the Carmanah–Walbran Park will help in the short term. But what happens when these areas become crowded? The wilderness experience that is a recognized need of the human soul may be greatly lacking.

To appreciate the effect of logging on an old-growth forest, it is important to understand its history and the changes that would be brought about if it were logged. In the coastal zone, the forest moves through several transitions, known as stages of succession, before it reaches its climax state, when it can reproduce itself. After a major fire (or clear-cut logging), the first species to recolonize the land are usually fireweed, shrubs and alder. These pioneer species are in great abundance on the Juan de Fuca Trail in the vicinity of Parkinson Creek. The pioneer stage is followed by Douglas-fir, which cannot regenerate in shade. As the Douglas-fir forest ages and dies, it is replaced by a cedar-hemlock forest, which regenerates itself, since the seedlings of these species are able to tolerate shade. Western cedar-hemlock is thus the climax forest of the west coast of southern Vancouver Island. A Douglas-fir forest is considered to be temporary. Along most of the eastern coast of Vancouver Island, fires have historically prevented the forest from reaching a climax stage. Logging now performs that same function in most parts of British Columbia outside of parkland. But on the island's west coast and in some of its valleys, fires are rare because of high rainfall, and many forests have evolved for thousands of years without interference.

Thus, the low-level climax forest is a multi-age forest, which may have taken up to two thousand years to evolve. This forest is characterized by enormous trees, limited undergrowth (which makes travel relatively easy) and a forest floor rich in small plants, mosses, ferns, lichens and many unusual fungi. Such a forest has been described as "decadent" or "overmature" by industrial foresters, because older trees grow slowly and contain a high proportion of rot. But such a forest also provides critical habitat for endangered species of wildlife such as spotted owls, marbled murrelets and spotted salamanders.

The replacement forest in a clear-cut has an entirely different character. For the first twenty years it is virtually impenetrable as the young trees grow. The bush tends to be thick salal, and berries such as salmonberry and blackberry abound. For the next twenty years the forest stand is still full of logging debris and the stems of young trees killed by competition with their neighbours. The richness of the forest floor is gone, logging debris impedes travel, and wildlife habitat is destroyed. Only in the last half of the cycle does the forest become attractive to the recreationalist. But the gigantic trees are gone forever.

Clear-cut logging also alters water quality and hydrodynamics. Without the large trees and their enormous root systems to hold the soil, topsoil is easily eroded by the rains and is washed out to sea. Along the way streams become filled with silt, and salmon habitat and spawning beds are destroyed. Incessant winter rains erode the rich humus needed to replenish life in the forest. Loss of humus not only makes it more difficult for trees to regenerate but also means that fewer nutrients are available to the entire ecosystem.

Graphic examples of clear-cut logging are all too evident on southern Vancouver Island. Along the way to the trailheads at Port Renfrew, Bamfield and the Carmanah–Walbran, extensive clear-cuts can be seen from the road—in stark contrast to the lush old-growth forests that wait once the hike is begun.

British Columbia is advertised as a tourist's paradise. Every year visitors flock here from many countries that have already logged their forests and have destroyed their wilderness. Tourists want to see the exceptional. The old climax forests of the Nitinat, along the West Coast Trail and in the Carmanah and Walbran Valleys are exceptional— MacMillan Bloedel and Timber West's uniform second-growth stands are not.

In the areas described in this book, the public has realized that these areas have special significance. In 1970, the Sierra Club of British Columbia began a campaign to make the public aware of the need to protect the West Coast Trail and environs. The club has also attempted to demonstrate that forest land has great recreational, scientific and spiritual value. The club has lobbied the provincial government vigorously and, through slide presentations, films, speeches and books, has attempted to educate the public about wilderness issues and values.

Conservationists in British Columbia must be vigilant to ensure that no encroachment of existing wilderness occurs. They must also continue to act to help set aside additional public lands for wilderness, scientific, ecological and recreational values. If these wilderness areas and old-growth forests are clear-cut, not only British Columbia but also the rest of the world will lose a valuable resource. One need only hike along the coastal trails or visit the giant trees in the Carmanah Valley to understand that these places are indeed sacred and ought to be preserved.

In part, this book has been written to help hikers enjoy the West Coast Trail area and to appreciate that wilderness is a priceless and endangered resource. Everyone who has hiked even a few kilometres of the hikes in this book has experienced the natural beauty of the area. If those thousands of hikers were moved to voice their support for wilderness and were to write letters to the provincial and federal governments urging that further wilderness areas be preserved, then the wilderness message of the West Coast Trail and environs may have its most profound effect. Your views are important and ought to be made known to the politicians who are responsible for deciding the future of British Columbia's wilderness.

The following addresses are provided so that you may voice your concern that the value of wilderness continue to be recognized.

National Parks Lands:
Minister of the Environment
Canadian Parks Service
Parliament Buildings
Ottawa, Ontario
KIA IG2

Provincial Lands:
Minister of Environment, Lands and Parks
Parliament Buildings
Victoria, B.C.
v8v 1x4

Minister of Forests
Parliament Buildings
Victoria, B.C.
v8v 1x4

For more information about wilderness issues in western Canada, or to forward comments or suggestions about this book, write to the Sierra Club of British Columbia, P.O. Box 8202, Victoria, B.C. v8v 2m6. The phone number is 250-386-5255.

For Further Reading

Gill, Ian. *Hiking on the Edge.* Vancouver: Raincoast Books, 1995.

Godman, Josephine E. *Pioneer Days of Port Renfrew.* Victoria: Solitaire Publishing, n.d.

Jones, Chief Charles. *Queesto-Pacheenaht Chief by Birthright.* Nanaimo: Theytus Books, 1981.

Kirk, Ruth. *Wisdom of the Elders.* Vancouver: Douglas & McIntyre, 1986.

Kozloff, Eugene N. *Seashore Life of the Northern Pacific Coast.* Seattle: University of Washington Press, 1983.

Macfarlane, J. M., H. J. Quan, K. K. Uyeda and K. D. Wong. *Official Guide to Pacific Rim National Park Reserve.* Calgary: Blackbird Naturgraphics, 1996.

McMillan, Alan D. *Native Peoples and Culture of Canada.* Vancouver: Douglas & McIntyre, 1995.

Nicholson, George. *Vancouver Island's West Coast 1762–1962.* Victoria: George Nicholson, 1965.

Obee, Bruce. *The Pacific Rim Explorer.* North Vancouver: Whitecap Books, 1985.

Pojar, Jim, and Andy MacKinnon, editors. *Plants of Coastal British Columbia.* Vancouver: Lone Pine Publishing, 1994.

Snively, Gloria. *Exploring the Seashore in British Columbia, Washington and Oregon.* West Vancouver: Gordon Soules Book Publishers, 1995.

Stoltmann, Randy. *Hiking the Ancient Forests of British Columbia and Washington.* Vancouver: Lone Pine Publishing, 1996.

Walbran, John T. *British Columbia Coast Names.* Vancouver: Douglas & McIntyre, 1971.

Wells, R. E. *A Guide to Shipwrecks along the West Coast Trail.* Victoria: Sono Nis Press, 1981.

Index